*Britney Spears' Heart to Heart*

# Britney Spears' Heart to Heart

Britney and Lynne Spears

with Sheryl Berk

SCHOLASTIC INC.

New York  Toronto  London  Auckland  Sydney
Mexico City  New Delhi  Hong Kong

ISBN 0-439-26301-8

12 11 10 9 8 7 6 5 4 3 2 1          0 1 2 3 4 5/0

Printed in the U.S.A.                         23

First Scholastic printing, October 2000

Design by Sarah Von Dreele

## To Sandra

*You're more than just a sister and an aunt; you're our inspiration.*

# contents

# acknowledgments

Many thanks to all the people who contributed their time and efforts to our book and who shared their wonderful memories: Sheryl Berk; Larry Rudolph; Mark Steverson; Johnny Wright; Frank Weimann; Felicia Culotta; Kristin Kiser and the staff at Crown; Jamie, Bryan, Blaize, and Jamie Lynn Spears; Sandra, Reggie, and Laura Lynne Covington; Jill Prescott; and finally, all the Kentwood folk. We couldn't have done it without y'all!

My mama, Lynne, lights up a room when she walks into it. She just radiates warmth, and it's the most wonderful feeling in the world to be around her. People are simply drawn to her, and the friends she has are her friends forever—and then some. That's why I'm so lucky that she's my best friend.

What we have between us is something rare. The older I get, the more I realize that. Growing up, I knew so many girls who used to fight all the time with their moms—over everything, it seemed: boys, clothes, curfews—and that used to make me so sad. I wished they could all have a mom like mine. (Although my brother, my sister, and I would've hated to share her with anyone else!) She is the strongest, bravest, most generous person I have ever known, and I'd be truly blessed if even just a little bit of that has rubbed off on me. An interviewer once asked me what I thought was the key to success. Well, I think it takes three very important things: (1) talent, (2) a belief in yourself, and (3) someone who believes in you. My mama was and is that someone.

I wanted to write this book so people could understand what a special bond we have between us and how much we've depended on each other over the years—through good times and tough ones (and there *have* been some tough ones). I hope that in sharing our story we'll inspire mothers and daughters to open their hearts to one another. It would also be great to be able to encourage kids to follow their dreams and not to be scared to set high goals. I'm living proof that you *can* succeed, no matter where you're from or how little you have. My family didn't have a whole lot of "things" when I was growing up, but we had one another.

Back home, folks always joke that my mama and I can complete each other's sentences. It's true—and besides that, she calls me at exactly the moment I need her most. Don't ask me how she does it. Somehow she senses what I'm feeling, even if we're thousands of miles apart.

So I'd tell her right now just how much I love her, but she already knows. ❀

*introduction*

Britney and I would go to the moon for each other. Mothers and daughters aren't always as close as we are, especially during the teenage years. It's a hard time, and there's potential for a lot of misunderstanding. People say there's a generation gap. Well, I don't really believe that. We've always managed to put any differences aside and focus on what is the key to any good relationship—love and respect for each other. You can love your child and you can love your mama (that's nature's way), but it is important to truly *like* your child and your mama, too.

Kids will make mistakes; they'll do things they shouldn't. That's a given. But didn't we all make mistakes when we were younger? I always try to remind myself of that and stay as open-minded as possible. (I just love it when Brit tells me I'm "cool.") Maybe I don't understand everything that she likes or does (the belly-button-piercing thing I just *do not get!*), but I give her room to learn, room to explore, room to grow. Which doesn't mean I don't worry—that's a mother's job, after all. But I know that she's got a good head on her shoulders and a big heart, and they'll be her guides when I can't be with her.

I certainly don't want any of the credit for Britney's success. She's earned that all by herself. I haven't done anything more for my daughter than any good mother would do: I just nurtured her on her path. I believed that Britney had a great gift and that she should use it, if that's what her heart was telling her to do. There were people along the way who told me I was doing the wrong thing, that I was building up her hopes and it could only lead to heartbreak. What kid from Kentwood, Louisiana, ever went on to become a pop star, much less by the age of seventeen? But just because no one had done it before didn't mean Britney couldn't. Someone had to be the first, so why not her? I knew there'd be plenty of obstacles in her path, and I tried my best to prepare her for them and help her jump those hurdles as they came along.

I'm an elementary-school teacher and I love to teach, so of course I'd like everyone to learn something from our experiences. This book is a wonderful chance for me to share some of the things I've learned while raising Brit, her brother, Bryan, and her little sister, Jamie Lynn. Lesson 1: Being a parent is more than just helping with homework, kissing scraped knees, or nursing the chicken pox. It's a lifelong job and it's the most challenging—yet the most rewarding—one you will ever have. Lesson 2: There's no book on how to be the perfect parent, no rules to follow. (And I'm thankful for that because I probably broke them all!) Every child is special and unique, and you just do the very best you can. And finally, Lesson 3: There is no greater joy than finding your meaning in life—except maybe helping someone you love find hers.

Writing this book with Brit has been a labor of love for both of us. We've shared so much over the past eighteen years, and we still do. (You should see our phone bills!) What I hope you take away from our efforts is a better understanding of who Britney is (who knows her better than her mama?) and of the power of love, faith, and family. If you believe in these things and follow your heart, the sky is the limit. ✿

Lynne Spears

*Britney Spears' Heart to Heart*

What an
adorable
pirate!

# Mama's Little Girl

Everyone in our family always seemed to have boys—my sister, Sandra, and my brother, Barry, both had sons; my husband Jamie's stepsiblings all had boys. We used to joke that we had enough males between us to start a baseball league!

Our first child was our son, Bryan, and growing up he was about as all-boy as you can get. He just loved sports, and he ended up becoming a karate expert, a champion football and basketball player, and a coach. He's now the director of a therapeutic facility for sports injuries. When Britney was born four years later, on December 2, 1981 (coincidentally, Sandra was pregnant at the same time with her daughter, Laura Lynne), you can imagine how excited I was: An adorable baby girl to dress up like a little doll! A daughter to have tea parties with! I'd braid her hair! Luckily for me, Brit loved being a girl. She collected dolls (even today, her room is filled with curio cabinets containing dozens of Madame Alexanders, porcelain dolls, and dainty miniature shoes), delighted in frilly clothes, and always seemed to get into her mama's makeup. But along with all that sugar there was also a bit of spice: Britney could be a handful.

One thing you should know about Brit: this desire to perform didn't just pop up overnight. She's probably been at it since the day she could walk. It's true. If you ask anyone who knew her while she was growing up in Kentwood, Louisiana, they'll tell you: even as an itty-bitty thing she was dancing to the music. She'd put on these shows for our family and friends and take her bows like a professional. (And God help you if you didn't just drop everything to watch her!) She was always a happy child, but it was performing that made her the happiest. I think she would have jumped off a roof if she thought it would get applause!

Of course, she didn't limit herself to just dancing. There was singing, too, and plenty of it. She would bounce on the trampoline while she was singing. She would jump rope while she was singing. She would stand on her head while she was singing. She would sing in the car, in the backyard, and even on my sister Sandra's kitchen table. But her favorite place to sing was the bathtub, because the acoustics were—as she would tell me—"awesome."

Everybody around home used to listen to country music. The big names were Dolly Parton, Loretta Lynn, Reba McEntire. It's a rural area with a population of only about two thousand people. There are lots of farms, horses and cows, green hills and red earth—so country music is what you're born and bred on, along with buttermilk biscuits, cornbread, and grits. But maybe because my mama was originally from England, I never really got into that sound. Instead I used to play pop. I would be driving in the car and

After nothing but boys in our family, you can believe my sister, Sandra, and I were thrilled to have little girls! Here we are with our mama. I am on the right, pregnant with Brit, and Sandra is in the middle, pregnant with Laura Lynne.

## *My Little Star*

*By Lynne Spears*

*Winter is gone,*
*Spring is here.*
*Life seems so good,*
*It's a new year.*

*She's the great gift,*
*A gift of spring.*
*You just enjoy watching—*
*She will dance and sing.*

*Cruel world, turn away,*
*Spare my little star.*
*Let her wit and charming beauty*
*Go very far.*

*There's a kindred spirit*
*That's thrilling to see.*
*The closeness that we feel—*
*It's so fulfilling to me.*

*[Written when Britney was just a toddler.]*

I'd crank up the Top 40 really loud. Britney just loved it. She'd sing along to Madonna, Michael Jackson, Whitney Houston, Mariah Carey. That's where her first vocal training came from. She could imitate any singer's style with absolutely perfect pitch.

And once we got her started, we couldn't get her to stop singing—although her brother, Bryan, her daddy, Jamie, and I would sometimes beg for a little peace and quiet! It was just a part of her; it was how she expressed herself. What a crazy house we had: Bryan would be on the roof pretending he was a ninja hunter while Brit would be singing and doing backflips around the living room. My children never did lack imagination!

Every preschool child has an outlet for his or her creativity. Maybe it's building huge cities out of blocks or outfitting dolls in outrageous ensembles or (God help you!) crayoning colorful pictures all over the walls. (Brit's little sister, Jamie Lynn, was great at that.) As a mother, you have to ask yourself: "With a little nurturing, could I have an architect, a fashion designer, or a budding Picasso on my hands?" Of course you'd love to think so; you're the proud mama or daddy, and it's hard to tell sometimes who has the greater fantasy life, the parent or the child. Recognizing talent isn't easy (why do you think all those casting directors in Hollywood get paid a lot of money?), and nurturing it is even tougher. Try talking a kid into practicing her piano scales when MTV's *Total Request Live* is on. You walk a very fine line. If you push too hard ("Practice your piano right now, young lady!") it becomes a chore and your child winds up hating it or, worse, hating you. But if you don't push at all, then how will that talent ever evolve?

So my advice is this: Ask your child if she really, truly, madly loves music or art or soccer or gymnastics or whatever. If she does—and if she's good at it—then help her to become even better. But always let it be her choice, not yours. And when the choice is between practice or catching the latest Backstreet Boys video, try a compromise: "Why don't you practice *after* you watch a little TV?" Then everyone is happy. ✿

*"Other kids would want to play with dolls; Britney wanted to sing and dance and put on plays. Somehow she always dragged me into them with her. It was no use arguing with her—she'd talk you into it."* —Kasie Smith, friend

# Applause, Applause

I was always acting out make-believe concerts in the bathroom. We had this great big mirror in there, and I'd stand on the edge of the tub (that was my stage), line up my dolls and stuffed animals on the floor (my adoring fans), grab a shampoo bottle (my microphone), and belt out a number. I would be checking myself out in that mirror, practicing my smile and blowing kisses to the crowd. I'd lock the door, too, so when my parents or my big brother were pounding on it, trying to get me to come out, it was no use. I'd be in there for hours and hours. I would pretend I was the biggest star in the world—bigger than Madonna, even. And I'd sing every lyric I knew (and even some I didn't) as loud as I could. "Brit-Brit, please keep it down!" Mama would plead. Bryan was more direct: "Britney, you'd better shut up right this minute!" But I knew better: the folks in the back rows of my giant imaginary concert arena needed to be able to hear me loud and clear!

I don't think my family paid much mind at first to my passion for performing. They just chalked it up to an overactive imagination and too much energy. But I remember when I was about three, I was jumping up and down on a trampoline out in the yard, singing a Sinéad O'Connor song, and my mother walked by. She stopped and stared. "Lordy, Brit," she finally said. "You can *really* sing!" She took me inside and had me perform the whole song for her and my brother, and they were pretty surprised. Later that day, I went to a gymnastics lesson, and Mama asked Miss Gigi, my teacher, to come listen to me sing along with the car radio. Miss Gigi's eyes got real big and Mama smiled, then said, "What did I tell you?"

I know that lots of little girls dream of becoming stars one day, and I'm not sure what made my mom realize this was anything more than some phase I was going through. Yes, I had talent, but there's a lot of talent out there. And talent, I can tell you, is not enough. It takes a whole lot more than the ability to carry a tune to make your dreams come true.

It takes a great support team. My family has always been there for me, right from the start. I'm really thankful to my parents. Usually, parents are the ones pushing the child, but in this case I was the one pushing them. They sacrificed a lot for me—especially my mama. She drove me to all my lessons, clapped harder than anyone (even when I messed up onstage; I always beat myself up about that!), and told me how proud of me she was. Anytime I'm down, I know who to call to pick me up—my mama. I get my optimism from her, and definitely my strength, because she was the one who first took me seriously and said, "Whatever you dream, you can do." I believed her. She always understood how important my goals were to me, and she never questioned them. ❖

"I was sitting in the Spearses' living room and I heard what I thought was the radio playing real loud. Turns out it wasn't the radio at all—it was Britney singing in the bathroom."

—Ginger Simmons, friend

Britney loved to sing, even as a little girl. At the age of four she entertained the graduating kindergartners and their folks at the school I ran.

Britney graduated at age five from kindergarten. I always taught her that school was as important as her singing and dancing.

# We're in This Together

I sensed right away that performing meant more to Britney than to most youngsters. She took it very, very seriously. When she was just three, she and her cousin, Laura Lynne, were in a dance recital together (I still remember those little tiaras and gold lamé leotards!), and Britney proceeded to tell all the little girls to get in a straight line—they were ruining the act! It wasn't that she was bossy (although maybe she was, just a little…), she just wanted her performance to be perfect. She always held very high standards for herself; she's never content being second-best.

Britney had a certain spark about her, too. She loved to pose. If you look at pictures of her when she's only a year or two old, she's got her hands on her hips, lips pouting, voguing for the camera. And when she came onstage, she knew how to command an audience. Her solo debut was at age four. She sang "What Child Is This?" in the preschool Christmas program at the Kentwood First Baptist Church. The whole town couldn't stop talking about how great she was. She just blew everyone away.

Right from the start I felt that if this was what she really wanted, I was going to do everything I could to help her achieve her dreams. But there was one big problem we had to deal with: our family had hardly a cent between us, and lessons were expensive. You always read these rags-to-riches stories and you think, "Oh, it couldn't have been that bad." Well, let me tell you: for us, it was worse than bad—it was plain awful!

In the beginning, things were okay. We had a house and a car and were living comfortably. Then in about 1990—and until as recently as a year or two ago—my husband Jamie's contracting business wasn't doing well. That made things tight. My little salary from the day care center or the school that I ran hardly helped much. Then also we had expenses for doctors and medicine, because when Bryan was little he had terrible asthma. He had a seizure once, and we actually had to airlift him to a hospital in New Orleans, which was very scary—and very expensive. The bills would come and we couldn't pay them; the power company threatened to turn off our lights, and the phone company went right ahead and cut off our service. Our heater broke and we couldn't afford to fix it, so for two winters we made do with these itty-bitty gasoline space heaters. (It was so cold sometimes you could see your breath.) The cupboards were often bare, and there were days when all we had in the fridge was a pint of ice cream.

We were always honest with our children about our financial situation. Jamie and I believe that when you're a family you don't keep secrets from one another: if there's a problem, it's everyone's problem. When they got a little older, Brit understood that if she wanted a new doll, she had to baby-sit to earn money to buy it. And if Bryan needed new sneakers for basketball, we'd have to start saving months ahead to be able to afford them come the season's start, and he'd have to help his granny out at her seafood restaurant to earn some money as well. There was no such thing as an allowance in our home. Are you kidding? Brit and Bry got $2.50 each day for lunch money, and even that was a struggle.

Maybe out of necessity, we learned to be creative. You know all those moms on TV who are always in the kitchen in those cute little aprons, baking cookies and brownies? Well, forget it. We couldn't afford many of the ingredients, so instead we'd make ice cream smoothies.

Britney liked to dress cool like the other girls in her class, so she became a genius at shopping the sale racks and discount stores and putting together fabulous outfits that looked like a million bucks but cost less than $20! Truth be told, I think that's how she developed her flair for fashion today. Labels still don't matter much to her—she's just as happy in a pair of old Levis as she is in a Chloé jumpsuit she might wear for an awards show. And like her mama, she loves a bargain!

I remember we had this little family meeting—Jamie, Bryan, Brit, and I—and we decided that no matter what it took, we'd get Britney the lessons she needed. We all believed in her that much. So we scrimped and saved and rolled pennies and we made sure those lessons could happen. All her teachers were understanding and patient. They always let me pay them a week or two late.

Looking back, I don't know how we managed, but somehow we did. Bad as it was, it taught us something: God helps those who help themselves. We came together as a family in our times of need, and just knowing that the five of us were in this together (not to mention all our kin and friends who were always offering us help and hand-me-downs) gave us the strength to see it through. The paint may have been peeling, the pipes leaking, and the furniture and carpeting falling apart, but when it came to love and support, we were the richest people in Kentwood. Britney didn't need a lot of money to dream about the future—dreaming is free, after all—and I'm glad our little girl set her goals so high. ✿

*"Britney was about seven and playing at my house. All I kept thinking was, 'Does this child ever sit still?'"* —Margaret Smith, friend

I just loved dancing, and my cousin, Laura Lynne (on the left), loved it too. Weren't we cute in one of our first dance recitals! (I think we were about six years old here.)

# Gotta Dance

What do you do when your child has dreams that seem bigger than what you can support, with either time or money? You have to think hard and decide whether the sacrifice is worth it. We felt it was. Other parents in our situation might have decided lessons were too expensive, and that would have been the end of it. But the way we saw it, our family was making an investment in Brit's future. How could we *not* help her realize her goals? It was so clear that Brit loved performing, and it would have broken my heart to get in her way. I always used to tell her, "Don't you worry about what it costs. Just do your very best." Dreams should never have a price tag on them. I believe that if you want something bad enough, you'll find a way to do it. And we did.

Britney started taking dance lessons at the Renee Donewar School of Dance in Kentwood when she was only about two. They were just a bunch of babies then, all dolled up in tutus and ballet shoes, twirling around to the music. During recitals most of them would cry or wander off the stage looking for their mamas, but not Brit. She did her little pirouettes and leaps and she pointed her toes; she waved her arms gracefully in the air, and at the end, to my thundering applause, she did a dainty curtsy. Miss Renee spotted right away that she had something special. Brit just loved her classes. She even won a Best Attendance award, and she'd cry something terrible if she had to miss a single lesson. When she was about six, it was suggested that we put her in a talent competition. So we did — just for fun. When she won it, I don't know who cried harder, her or me.

At the time, we also entered her in a beauty pageant. So many little girls were doing them. But I was appalled at what I saw: all these mothers telling their daughters that appearance was the most important thing in the world! I felt it was terribly unhealthy for children, and after that I never let Brit do another one. When she asked me why (I think she liked the idea of dressing up in pretty clothes and wearing makeup), I said, "Honey, I don't ever want you to think that what you see on the outside is more important than what you've got on the inside." And what kind of message were these girls getting when they didn't win? They all walked away thinking, "I'm not pretty enough." When you lose a talent competition, there's always room for improvement; it encourages you to practice more and work harder. But when you lose a beauty pageant, what can you work harder at? Being more beautiful? I think such things can shatter a child's self-image and confidence for life.

What was I going to do with all of Brit's gymnastics trophies? All my kids have brought home trophies and awards throughout the years. It sure makes a mama proud.

I guess I thought for a while that I was going to be a world-class gymnast, but I really loved to dance and just couldn't do both. Sometimes a girl just has to make a decision about what to do in life!

When Brit was around seven, she started really excelling in her tumbling. So in addition to the dancing classes, she took gymnastics. Her lessons were in Covington, which was an hour away, and I'd drive her five days a week. I was working at the time, running the day care center, and it was so hard. We were always running to one lesson or another. Everybody in the neighborhood would pitch in—they'd watch over Bryan while I was out, or they'd drive Britney when I couldn't.

With just a little practice, she began to shine in gymnastics. She won her level at the Louisiana State gymnastics meet. (That's where she first performed her now-famous backflips!) Her teacher recommended that we take her to another coach, and soon the lessons became much stricter and more demanding. One day I was driving her home and I could see that she was miserable. I said, "Britney, honey, what is it? What's wrong?" and she said, "Mama, I don't want to do this anymore. It's too hard." She wanted to give up gymnastics and focus only on dance.

I didn't know what to do. Should I encourage her to stick with it? She was at the top of her group, so I knew this wasn't about fear of failure. I wanted her to be happy, but everyone had told us how talented she was and what a bright future she could have—maybe even gold medals if she worked at it.

What helped me along was that I had already been through something similar with Bryan. There wasn't a sport he wasn't good at it, but he quit baseball to play football and basketball. That was his personal preference. And this was Britney's. ❁

"In elementary school, I'd line the kids up in gym class for relay races. Britney could outrun every girl. Then I'd line her up against the boys and she was faster than all of them, too. She just loved a challenge."

—Pam Spiers, Parklane Academy coach

# Do Your Own Thing

I think my mom was worried that this was just a temporary thing—that I was quitting because I'd had a bad day or I was feeling tired and I'd change my mind later on. Kids can be fickle and a little flaky like that sometimes. Not me. I always knew exactly what I wanted, even when I was little. I knew gymnastics wasn't for me because it wasn't fun anymore. These girls would weigh themselves after class, and if they were just one pound overweight they would freak. *Thanks, but no thanks.* Even though I was naturally skinny, I liked to eat! I knew the practice would get harder, not easier. That would have been okay if I were really and truly into it. But it never made me feel the way performing did.

I love that vibe when an audience is into my music, singing and clapping along. Sometimes when I'm up onstage, the lights on me are so bright that I can't make out a single face in the crowd. But I can *feel* them. There's no greater joy for a performer than knowing your audience can relate to what you're putting out there. It's like an instant connection, and it's powerful and fulfilling at the same time. I loved it back then, and I love it now. You've got to go with what makes you happy.

You know what I mean: All of us have experienced that rush of joy from doing something we're good at. Maybe you get a great high from scoring the winning goal in the game or landing the lead in the school play. Maybe solving an impossibly tough math equation is the ultimate. Whatever gives you that feeling of being on top of the world is what you should go for—and it doesn't necessarily have to be what your friends are into. While a lot of my friends liked gymnastics, that wasn't why I first got into tumbling, and I didn't worry about my friends either when I quit gymnastics to focus on dance. It just felt right to me at the time, and today I know I made the right decision. ❈

*"Once Britney makes up her mind to do something, look out! You'd better believe she's gonna do it. Just stand back and give my sister some room."* —Bryan Spears, big brother

You'd never know it from this picture, but Brit was usually pretty scared of Santa when she was little. Although I remember she liked the presents he brought!

# A Mom's Dilemma

Every parent feels a kind of tug-of-war at some point: How hard do you push if you see that your daughter has a gift? How much should you encourage her to explore it? I worried that I was doing Britney an injustice by letting her abandon gymnastics. At nine years old, how could she possibly have the ability to make such decisions? But what it boils down to is this: You have to know your child and you have to trust his or her instincts. The biggest mistake you can make is *not* taking heed of what he or she is feeling. You know, I beat myself up for months worrying about the "what ifs" and "what might have beens." But there is one thing we both learned from this experience: To be a success in anything, your heart has to be in it 100 percent, you have to have the drive and the burning desire, and doing it has to make you feel excited and happy and alive.

If you're ever wondering whether those ballet lessons or art classes or karate courses are right for your child, whether you should urge your little one to continue or not, talk to him or her about it. The best thing to do is ask *why* your child wants to quit ("I'm too lazy" is not a good enough answer) and guide him or her accordingly. In Jamie Lynn's case, she loves gymnastics and she's accomplished at it, but last year she suddenly decided she wanted to stop taking lessons. Well, we talked it over, and it turned out her reason was that her other little friends were in a different class. So we switched her to that one and now she couldn't be happier. I think the key when your kid wants to call it quits is to keep your cool and communicate. Yelling and threatening solves nothing.

With Britney, I just had to look at her to know I did the right thing in letting her switch directions. She was a very shy child, so seeing her onstage was like watching a transformation. Offstage she was afraid of her own shadow—not to mention spiders and Santa Claus. But in the spotlight she was a different person, brave and outgoing, with this big personality. You see, it was like playing a part to her: she wasn't Britney, she was someone else. But that only happened if she had a song to perform or a script to read. If she had to speak about herself in public, we were in big trouble. I remember when I'd ask her to introduce herself to the audience before her routines, she'd beg, "Oh, Mama, no! Don't make me do it!" She couldn't even say her name without turning red-faced. But when the music started, she'd come alive, all smiles and energy and charm. In the very beginning, I would coach her on the gestures to accompany the songs. Then suddenly she didn't need that anymore—she just interpreted it herself. She knew how to sell it. She was such a ham! I'd stare up at the stage and wonder, "Could that be my Britney?" The shyness had just vanished. ✿

"I think Brit gets a lot of her strength from her mama. Lynne is the kind of person who lets nothing stand in her way—not even a car that won't go (she'll just get out and push it) or bills piled up to the ceiling. Both of them believe that you take life's lemons and just make lemonade out of them." —Margaret Smith, friend

"She is so cool, and she's a really good singer and sister. When I grow up, I'm gonna be just like her." —Jamie Lynn Spears, little sister

# Even Stars Get the Jitters

I'd be lying if I said I never was nervous before a big competition or show. In those few minutes before the curtain went up or the announcer introduced me, I could feel my knees knocking. Sometimes I still do! But then I kind of go on autopilot. I just start to sing and dance, and the butterflies fly away. Maybe it's because I'm so focused. As long as you're concentrating on doing what you're supposed to be doing, you don't have time to worry. I also feel the energy of the audience, and that picks me up, too. When everyone is cheering for you, it's impossible to not get swept up in it. I'm having such a good time, I forget to stress out.

I've always been able to work through my fears and doubts. The way I see it, you can let them hold you back, or you can tell them to back off. It's all up to you. ❧

# Beyond Her Years

Britney has always been mature for her age. Our friend Felicia calls her an "old soul." I'd often wonder, "How could someone so young be so wise?" Not many children are capable of demonstrating such discipline, and to tell you the truth, I don't know where it comes from. Surely not from me! I always *say* I'll get to the gym, but I only make it if I'm lucky. I write myself a long list of things to do and then I only check off half of them.

Brit would practice her dances for hours and hours in the living room and she'd do her cartwheels right across our front lawn. (Our neighbors the Stricklands and the Reeds would come out of their houses to cheer her on.) If it sometimes meant missing her favorite TV shows, *The Wonder Years* and *Growing Pains*, that was okay by her. She was dedicated. She was also the most organized little thing. She kept all her clothes in neat piles: pants here, skirts there, shirts somewhere else—all in perfect order. And every night she'd lay out her school outfit for the next day. I never had to tell her to make her bed or clean up her room. She just did it. ❧

# Balancing Act

I still feel guilty if I go home and don't make my bed in the morning. (That's at home, but you should see the mess I make when I'm on the road!) I guess I grew up seeing how disciplined Bry was about his sports and how into exercise my mama was. (She may *say* she doesn't stay in shape, but I remember she never missed a single day at the gym.) She worked at a health club for a while, and she would go every day and teach aerobics. When I was twelve, she and I even choreographed aerobics routines together and then showed everyone how to do them.

Maybe I tried to act grown-up because I wanted people to take me seriously, but don't get me wrong: I was completely capable of goofing around, too. Come weekends, I was over at Laura Lynne's or she was over at my place; we played with our Barbie dolls or rode go-carts. My parents made sure that even though I was dedicating a lot of my time to practicing, I was also making time to be just a regular kid. I don't feel as if I missed out on my childhood. I think that would have been a terrible thing, because kids should be kids.

I know that my little sister, Jamie Lynn, wants to follow in my footsteps and I think that's great. She has an amazing voice, and I have no doubt she'll be a big star one day. (She has no doubt, either!) But I've told her to take it slow—she's only eight, and I think she needs to enjoy being eight for a while. Then nine… I think kids should go to school, read, try lots of new things first. Take it from me, performing is not all glamour and limos and parties. It's a lot of hard work, and you have to be prepared for that, both in mind and in spirit. If you think you are, then by all means you should go for it. But make sure you don't miss out on all the fun stuff. You're not a kid for very long, so you should enjoy it. ❀

*"She has this sweet innocence. I could persuade her it's going to rain little dogs tomorrow and she'd say, 'Yes, ma'am.' She has the most trusting heart."* —Margaret Smith, friend

Laura Lynne has been there for me from the day we were born. We were just three years old in this picture!

*Just look at what our mamas did to me and Brit when we were little. They took every opportunity to dress us alike!*

### **Best Buddies** Laura Lynne Covington

*Britney and I have been the best of friends since the day we were born. Our mamas are sisters, and Britney has always been just like a sister to me. Every Christmas they'd buy us the same nightgowns—we were so adorable! But you should see some of the embarrassing pictures they have of us. Brit and I have tried hiding them, but it's no use!*

We were always taking dancing lessons together: we both love to dance. I remember a lot of times looking over and seeing Brit next to me in a recital and thinking how great she was. (I swear we were in diapers for our very first one!) I always knew she had an incredible gift. I never doubted for one minute that she would be a star one day, though I hardly think of her like that.

To me she's just Britney. She doesn't put on any airs or act differently, even though her life has changed so much these past few years. When she's home, we're hangin' out like the old days, goofin' around, talking about boys and clothes and who's going to what college. We have the greatest memories of growing up together. We've shared practically everything (especially clothes), and that's a bond we'll never break.

Everyone is always asking me what Britney's **really** like—reporters, fans, people who might have seen her on MTV or at some awards show. She's exactly the way she seems: sweet, kind, fun, talented. It's not an act—and I've known her for eighteen years, so I'm an **expert** on Miss Britney. I think that's why audiences are so drawn to her. She's the real thing, the whole package. What you see is what you get. ✿

"We went to New York with the best attitude: Let's have fun. And fate just came right along and found Britney, as it always does."

—Jeannine Ballard, aunt

*Chapter 3*
*Blessings in Disguise*

# Not Old Enough

Even though I am so focused and have always known what I've wanted to do, I would occasionally be surprised when things didn't happen the way I thought they would. And then I'd be even *more* surprised when this turned out to be a *good* thing. I remember I was eight the first time I auditioned for *The All-New Mickey Mouse Club* (also known as *MMC*). I was always into Disney and I thought it would be so cool to be on TV, but I didn't really feel any pressure. "If I get this, that would be fun," I thought, "but if not, okay then."

I remember they were holding casting calls in Atlanta, so that's where we had to travel. There were probably thousands of kids who wanted the spots on the show, and only about a dozen of them would make it. I sang and danced my little heart out for the directors. I even did some pretty impressive cartwheels, which I thought would make me a shoo-in. But what it boiled down to was that I was still too young and inexperienced: most of the Mouseketeers were at least twelve and already had long résumés.

In the long run, it turned out that being rejected was a good thing. Imagine that! One of the casting directors was impressed (like I said, it must have been those cartwheels) and gave me the name of a good agent in New York City. So we took the address and phone number, and off we went to the Big Apple on our first big adventure.

New York seemed like a world away from Kentwood (I remember asking Mama if they had any cows there), but it was the center of everything. If you want to be a performer, the city is the place to be. I was pretty fearless about leaving home. I knew I'd miss my family and friends, but I put that out of my mind. Besides, this wouldn't be forever: it was just a stepping-stone. I wasn't getting off track; I was going to be following another path that would still take me to what I wanted to do—perform. ❀

*Here I was, a little girl in the big city. I am sure glad my mama was with me when I was in New York. We missed Kentwood, but we had each other.*

# Leaving It All Behind

"Lynne, you must be out of your mind, taking your baby to that big city where who-knows-what will happen!" That's what a lot of neighbors in Kentwood were saying to me when we headed out to New York to get Britney an agent. People thought it was such a shot in the dark and that by starting Britney on her career so early we were depriving her of her childhood. They thought we should just put her dreams on the back burner till after she finished high school. But in this business (we know this now), time is of the essence. Besides, if we hadn't helped her on her way when she wanted it, we would have been stifling her. I think a lot of the opposition we got had to do with the small-town way of thinking: "It's better to stay where you are and how you are than ever try to change things."

But big cities didn't scare me one bit, and Brit was determined to break into performing. So off we went—me, Brit, her daddy, Bryan, and his buddy Hunter (we wanted him to have a friend along so he wouldn't be bored), my husband's sister, Jeannine, and her little girl, Tara. We couldn't afford airfare (it was more than $400 a person), so we took Amtrak—twenty-six hours on a train! We all stayed in one hotel room because that was what we could pay for.

Compared to the quiet dirt roads of Louisiana, the concrete streets of New York were loud and bright and a bit overwhelming. But we had the best time running around, although I was very pregnant then with Jamie Lynn, and I waddled more than ran. We couldn't afford cabs, so we'd walk most places, even in the pouring rain. (Picture seven people huddled under one umbrella!) We treated our trip as a vacation and a chance to see new sights and meet new people. There was really no pressure for Brit to land any part at all. But you know, she did. ❋

# Give My Regards to Off-Broadway

New York actually became my second home for a while. Mama stayed with me along with Jamie Lynn, who was just a baby. For three summers, I studied at The Professional Children's School (you had to audition to get in and be working in theater, movies, TV, or music to enroll) and at the Broadway Dance Center. I was picked to be the understudy for the lead in the off-Broadway show *Ruthless!* at The Players Theatre. I played Tina, a little girl who looks sweet and innocent but is really the devil in disguise. It was a lot of fun to play her because she couldn't have been more the opposite of me: Tina is spoiled rotten and she would kill (literally) to be a big star.

Even though the part was fun, the process of doing the same thing night after night wasn't. It got a little boring for me. As an understudy, I had to be at every performance whether I got to go on or not (and I only got to go on when the star was sick, which was hardly ever). I had to know every line by heart so I'd be ready at a moment's notice. I eventually did get the role when the original actress left, but by then I was growing tired of it and was eager to move on myself. ❁

# Stepping Out

What Britney loved most about those years in New York were her dancing lessons. She has always had an incredible memory. She could learn a dance routine faster than anyone else. Show her a combination of steps, and she could get it right off the bat. It came naturally to her. When she was studying at the Broadway Dance Center, the teacher would always put her in front of all the other students to lead—and she was just nine years old and there were people in the studio who were three times her age! She soaked it all up, everything they taught her. She'd watch a grown-up do some fancy jazz routine and she'd squeal, "Let me try! I want to do it, too!" And she would—just as well, if not better. The Broadway Dance Center was a far cry from the studio she'd been in back home: the people who studied at the school were some of the best in the business. (Brit still likes to work on the routines for her videos and concerts there.) So when we left New York, she had grown both literally (about three inches) and as a dancer as well. I kept thinking, "Wait till they get a look at her now."

We owe a big thank-you to that casting director who turned Brit down for *MMC*, although we didn't feel very thankful at the time. It just goes to show you that sometimes wonderful opportunities can spring up from disappointments. That means being brave and, most important, being flexible. So you didn't make the cheerleading squad. Hey, maybe there's an opening in the chorus for a girl with a big voice. The coach puts you in the outfield instead of on the pitcher's mound. Maybe you can catch that fly ball that saves the game.

I always tell Brit that God works in mysterious ways. If you're looking in one direction and the path ends, then turn around and see where other roads might lead you. One of these roads may be the right one, the one you were meant to take. It's okay to shift gears now and then: New York was not what we had bargained for, but it was a great experience, and it certainly led to many more. You always need to look for the one good thing, the one lesson to pull out of any situation. ❁

## Brotherly Love *Bryan Spears*

*When Britney got to be a teenager, I made sure I watched over her whenever my parents couldn't. One night when she was maybe thirteen or fourteen, she decided to sneak out and go with a few of her girlfriends over to some boy's house in McComb, a town nearby. Well, my friend and I followed them, and of course we tattled. Britney got grounded but good! Her punishment was walking around the neighorhood with a bucket and picking up trash on the ground for the whole day. She cried the whole time and of course I took pictures of her—just so she wouldn't forget what happens when you break curfew!*

In high school all these boys were wanting to ask her out, but they had to get not just Daddy's approval but mine as well. I was a big football player, so I think a lot of them chickened out because they were afraid of me.

Now, when I see her all grown up and on these magazine covers, looking all glamorous, I hate it and I tell her so. I say, "Take that goop off your face; you look ridiculous!" I understand it—it's part of the business—but it's fun to tease her all the same.

*I know I don't look big enough here to intimidate any of Brit's potential dates, but wait until I got to high school!*

Whenever she comes home now, it's the same Britney. We fight. I'm the only person who knows what to say to her to get her real steamed—and that's fun. But she is a lot more responsible than she used to be. I see that in her. And you can bet I'm proud of my baby sister. ❋

I tried to help Brit with everything I could while she was growing up, whether it was curling her hair for her appearance on **Star Search** or giving her a shoulder to cry on when she didn't win that day.

# And the Winner Is...

We have a three-bedroom, two-and-half-bath ranch house in Kentwood—nothing fancy, just wood and brick—and almost every inch of it is covered with the blue ribbons and trophies (and now, quite a few music awards and platinum records!) that Brit and Bryan have won over the years. When Britney was young, she won first place in the Kentwood Dairy Festival—she did a number with a top hat and cane à la Fred Astaire. Then we took her to the Miss Talent Central States Competition in Baton Rouge, where she won again. Each time she won, she got a little check, which we used to pay for more lessons, costumes, and trips to more talent shows. Her biggest prize at that point was for Miss Talent USA—she won a tiara, a trophy that I swear was taller than she was, and a $1,000 check. Shortly after that, when she was ten, she was chosen to appear on TV as a contestant on *Star Search*.

I think, in her mind, Brit had gotten used to all this winning. She'd show up at a talent contest and the other little girls would moan, "Oh, no, it's Britney Spears, there goes first prize!" So why wouldn't she feel as if she could win over and over again? Maybe she'd even come to expect it a little because it always came to her so easily. It's kind of like when you have a Little League team with a perfect season and then suddenly, out of nowhere, they lose a game. Well, it knocks the wind right out of you!

Of course, there isn't much you can do as a parent to prepare your child for that disappointment. You certainly don't want to take the wind out of her sails by being the voice of gloom and doom. You want her to enjoy every exciting moment of her successes and not worry about failure. But we all know that no one can win all the time—life just isn't like that. The best you can do is explain to your child that it's not whether you win or lose, but how you play. (I know that sounds like a big cliché, but it's true.) And if that doesn't prepare your child enough, I strongly recommend lots of hugs and sympathy, because you know it's inevitable: one day, usually sooner rather than later, you're going to have to help your child deal with defeat. ❋

# All Eyes on Me

I was so excited about *Star Search* because it was on TV, and that meant people all over the country would be watching me. The way it went, you got about three minutes to do a little performance—in my case, a big, showstopping song that would highlight my range and how powerful my voice was. Four celebrity judges would rate your performance with stars, and if you had the most points, you became the champion. You had to keep coming back and doing a different number each time, until either you made it into the semifinals and finals or you got beaten.

The first time I was on, I won. I beat this little girl who sang opera. I got three and three-quarters stars, four being perfect, and she got three and a half. Ed McMahon, the show's host, joked around with me: he asked if I had a boyfriend back home and when I said no, he asked if he would do. I told him I'd have to think about it! Can you imagine?

The next round, I knew the boy I was up against, and he was so sweet. We actually had gone to the same school, The Professional Children's School in New York City, and we had played basketball together right before the show. I remember I went onstage and I just gave it my all. I sang this great song by Naomi Judd, "Love Can Build a Bridge," and I thought, "Wow, I feel really good about this performance." When Ed announced that my challenger had beaten me (by only a quarter of a star), I remember I gave that boy a big hug. Then I walked offstage and burst into tears. I went over and over it again in my head. What had I done wrong? The boy who'd won felt so bad for me, and so did my mama. I'd wanted to win so badly, and I knew everyone back home was watching me and I had let them down. How could I face them? ❁

# Words of Comfort

I just took Britney aside and said, "Now, baby, you have to be happy for that little boy and you have to be a good sport." She tried so hard to stop the tears—she didn't want Ed McMahon or anyone to see her cry, but she couldn't control it. Her heart was just broken.

But she got over it eventually, and it wouldn't be the first disappointment we'd have to face. There were many more over the years: endless auditions that didn't amount to anything; people who were jealous or insecure and wouldn't give Brit her due; others who said they'd help us but instead took our time and money and never came through. It doesn't even pay to rehash all the headaches, but there were plenty, and each time one came up, I'm proud to say, we never let it stand in our way. You have to keep your chin up, I'd always tell Brit. It's not the end of the world not to get *exactly* what you want.

All of those times pale in comparison to the biggest obstacle we had to deal with. Ironically, it came just when Britney had hit the top of the charts with her first single. It threw us all for a loop, but this time it was her mountain to climb alone. I couldn't do it for her, although had it been possible I would have taken her place without hesitation. There is nothing worse when you're a parent than seeing your child in pain.

# I Will Survive

The timing could not have been worse. I was in rehearsals for my second video, "Sometimes," when I did a high kick and felt something in my knee go *pop*. I was in a lot of pain, and I knew something was very, very wrong. Everyone kept trying to calm me down. They told me if I just iced it, it would be fine, but I could hardly bend it at all and I was terrified. I was crying hysterically and everyone thought I was overexaggerating. I was like, "Y'all, I can't stand on it!" I know my body, and I knew this was serious.

I called my mom and she called one of my managers, Larry Rudolph, and they got me to a doctor right away, who advised me to calm down and let it heal on its own. But it wasn't getting better; in fact, it was getting worse. So I went to a second doctor in New Orleans and he took one look at my X ray and said, "You need surgery as soon as possible. You have a piece of bone floating around in your knee."

*Here I am in the "...Baby One More Time" video. This was such an exciting time for me! I just couldn't believe I hurt my knee so badly, so soon after I made this video.*

*Dear Britney,*

*I heard you had to go to the hospital because you hurt your leg.*

*I am so sorry! I am your biggest fan and I hope you are okay. Everyone in my school here is hoping for you, too, because we think you are the best singer and dancer ever. We listen to "...Baby One More Time" all the time...it is our favorite song.*

*Please, please get better soon! You can do it, Britney!!!*

*Love,*

*Ricky P., Paramus, NJ*

I don't think the words registered at first. Surgery? Now? "…Baby One More Time" had just taken off, and everyone wanted me to be out there promoting, doing the talk-show rounds, making appearances. I couldn't disappear! But the doctor insisted I had no choice, so I had to cancel everything—appearances on *The Tonight Show with Jay Leno* here in the States and *Bravo* in Germany, and dozens of interviews.

It would take eight long and painful weeks of me being at home, resting my leg and going in for physical therapy. I was devastated. This could not be happening. Not now! The recovery was excruciating. I would lie on a bed and the therapists would stretch my leg out every day, bending it to make sure the ligaments and muscles were healing correctly. It hurt so bad I cried every time. The doctors told me that grown men who had to go through this screamed and cried, too, so it was okay to let it out. My mama stayed with me, holding my hand and telling me, "Hang in there, baby." Jamie Lynn tried her hardest to take my mind off it and make me laugh.

Even worse than the therapy was having to stay still all the time. I have lots of energy, and I couldn't do more than lie on the couch. I had to elevate my knee and stay off of it as much as possible. Let me tell you, it was torture. I think what got me through this horrible time was my attitude: I was just determined to get my knee back to the way it was. I can remember only one day, in the very beginning, when I thought about the worst possibility: What if I was never able to dance again? What if my whole career, everything that I had worked so hard for and was finally happening for me, was suddenly over? What if I didn't recover 100 percent? The doctors were always so positive and reassuring, but they did warn us that there was a slight risk of complications.

I cried on my mama's shoulder and she promised me it would all be okay if I was strong. So I was—for both our sakes—and every time those thoughts crept into my head, I chased them away. I had so much to look forward to, so much waiting for me—I had to get back. I worked harder than I've ever worked to build my knee up. The doctors were impressed with my progress and, even more than that, with my motivation.

Before I knew it, I started to get better. I could kick and bend, and before long I was doing those backflips. I would not ever want to go through something that painful again, but I learned something from it: The Lord and your mind can sometimes have the power to heal you. If you believe you will get better, that's half the fight right there. And my family, friends, and fans were so strong for me. Mama never let me see the worry in her eyes. Knowing I had people behind me, rooting for me, praying for me…it made all the difference in the world. ❁

Hurting my knee really made me realize how much I love performing. Lordy, I'd be crazy if I couldn't dance anymore!

Britney and I love my sister, Sandra, so much. She truly is an inspiration to us. Here she is with her daughter, Laura Lynne, in 1986.

You need kin in your life for love and support. That's what I've always told Brit, Bryan, and Jamie Lynn. Here I am with Sandra (at left) and our brother, Barry, in 1996.

# Our Hero

Right now, my sister Sandra—whom Britney and I love so dearly—is battling ovarian cancer. She has this incredible spirit: I have never seen her for one second give in to self-pity or fear or despair. She is so, so strong, and I truly believe that she'll get through this—with God's help—because she has a great attitude. These ladies in our family, you just can't keep them down for very long!

When Britney comes home, she can't wait to go see her aunt Sandra. They are both so proud of each other. I hate to brag about Brit in public—I don't want to sound like a show-off—but Sandra will not hesitate to stop anyone, anywhere, and say, "Have you heard about my niece? Isn't she amazing?" I've been in malls with her and she'll be telling Britney stories to total strangers! She can't help it—she's just bursting with pride.

When we started writing this book, Sandra was undergoing chemotherapy. It's not an easy thing to go through, and I think helping us recall all our family stories was the best medicine in the world for her. "Hey, Lynne," she'd say. "You remember that time when Britney and Laura Lynne climbed up in that tree?" Or, "Hey, you wanna watch that video of her being interviewed on the local news when she was eleven?" Mention Britney's name and her eyes just light up. If I ever doubted the power of the heart, I don't now. I see Sandra getting stronger and healing every day because she has so many people who love her.

No odds are ever unbeatable. You just ask Aunt Sandra. Our whole family truly believes that God gives us obstacles so we can learn from them. (I like to think of them as tests like you'd have in school.) Each time you overcome one, you get a little stronger, a little more sure of yourself, and you see things much more clearly. Soon those big rocks that used to block your path...well, they're no more than itty-bitty pebbles. ❁

*"Sometimes Britney will say something and it reminds me exactly of Lynne when she was that age. Even the way she says it! They're just two of a kind."* —Sandra Covington, aunt

This is Brit and me just as she was getting to be a teenager. The glamorous outfits were to come!

# Try, Try Again

I don't think for one minute that my family or I ever had a set plan about how my life would turn out. If there had been an outline to follow—we'll do this, then we'll do that, let's follow A, B, C, then D—I know for sure I would have failed or else been miserable. We just rolled with it, tried new things, took chances, and most of all had a great time along the way. I'm a firm believer that everything is in God's hands and you don't always know what's around the corner. If you knew exactly what lay ahead, what kind of an adventure would it be? If life were so predictable, wouldn't it be boring?

My lessons led to talent competitions, and that led to auditions, and eventually we wound up in New York. Our philosophy was really "Hey, why not?" I never felt any pressure. It was all about having fun and seeing where fate would take us.

There were so many times when things just didn't work out the way we had hoped (I *didn't* get on the *Mickey Mouse Club*) and times when we got some nice surprises (I *did* get on the *Mickey Mouse Club*!). We lost some, we won some. That's just the way it went in the basketball games I used to play in junior high school (I hated when we got our butts kicked, but it happens) and that's the way it goes in life, too. I could have given up; the second I'd have said "I'm done!" my mama would have happily packed our bags and took me back home. In fact, we did once: after six months of doing *Ruthless!* off-Broadway, I got homesick. It was close to the holidays and I hadn't been back to Kentwood at all; I missed my big brother and my daddy and all of my friends and family. Mama was feeling the same way, but neither of us wanted to say anything. We had a little mini Christmas tree in our apartment, but you know it just wasn't the same as the big evergreen we always had in our living room back home. I was so upset! I wouldn't be unwrapping presents under the tree with Bry, or going to our church on Christmas morning.

Then one day I just looked at Mama and said it. I said what we both were thinking: "Can't we go home for Christmas?" And just like that, we picked up and got on that plane. There was no doubt in our minds that family came first, and home is where you should be at the holidays. Even today, no matter where I am on tour, I make sure I'm home for Christmas Eve. I guess we both trusted that as long as this was what our hearts were telling us to do, we were making the right decision. The people in the play understood and, shortly after, I got cast on *MMC*. So there you go—it was all part of God's plan for me, anyway.

Around the same time, I also went on this audition for a movie called *Gordy*. I was offered the lead (opposite a *pig*, I kid you not) and my daddy was convinced this would be a great opportunity for me. Well, I didn't know about that. I was kind of afraid of all those animals, and honestly, I was holding out for *MMC*. So after lots of family discussions (and Mama defending my choice), we let the offer go. Let me tell you, I am so glad, because the movie wasn't a big hit.

It's important to stick up for what you believe in, even if others challenge you. I think when you begin to doubt yourself, it's like self-sabotage. As long as you're being true to your goals and working real hard, you have to have faith that everything will fall into place. And if it doesn't right away, you still have to keep on going. You can cry over something you can't control, you can sit there moping, feeling sorry for yourself, or you can just pick yourself up and try again. I did my share of crying, but it never lasted very long. Mama's optimism is contagious, and I guess my hopes were stronger than my fears. ❖

*"Lynne thinks ice cream can fix anything. You're depressed, you're mad, you're stressed out—well, you just go buy yourself a nice big ol' pint and you'll feel better in no time! Well, you know what? It worked every time for Britney, and I swear it still does."*

—Jill Prescott, friend

## Lynne's Love Letters

*I always give my family and friends poems on special occasions—birthdays, graduations, weddings—or simply for no reason, just to tell them how much I love them. Sometimes when we're traveling, Brit and I write poems together. (Maybe one day they'll wind up as lyrics in one of her songs.) This one in particular sums up our philosophy on faith and taking chances.*

*The birth of a new horizon,*
*Dawning of a new day.*
*Will the birds sing?*
*Or will the sky be gray?*

*There is no promise;*
*In life, one must not know.*
*If the path were easy,*
*One could not grow.*

# Everything in Time

I tell my kids: When God closes one door, He opens another. For Britney, that was always the case. I wouldn't characterize us as conventionally religious people, but we're certainly deeply spiritual. I was raised as a Methodist; attended a Catholic high school; and was married Baptist. So I have no certain religious protocol. But I believe that everything in life happens for a reason—the good things and even the bad ones. I used to tell Brit, "How would you know what a happy time was if you hadn't experienced a sad one?"

I think the disappointments we had were all part of God's great plan for her. She found her way when she was ready to handle all of this. Looking back now, I can see why landing *MMC* when she was eight and moving to Orlando wouldn't have been right: Bryan was too young to be away all the time from his mama, and Britney had lessons to learn in New York, onstage in *Ruthless!* When she did become a Mouseketeer three years later, Bryan was already driving and much more grown up, and she was more poised and professional. She was going to be able to get much more out of the experience at age eleven than she would have as a real young one. The timing was just right.

You have to see each obstacle as an opportunity to learn and grow. Not everything is revealed to us right away—sometimes you just need to have patience. (And patience is not even one of Brit's best virtues!) I always tried to make light of things for her. If she lost a competition, then I'd say, "So what? Let's go have some fun now, let's go get an ice cream." Judging is so subjective. You never know what someone's personal tastes will be. So I'd say, "Now, Brit, you know and I know you were the best, but it's all in the eye of the beholder." If I had been one of those stage mothers who's so demanding and has such high expectations, she would have been crushed by every little setback. She'd always look to me for my reaction—if I was okay with it, then she was okay with it. And I really was, because I knew that everything would somehow work out for the best.

I know people who say, "Why take chances? Why put yourself at risk? Why rock the boat at all?" Why? Because you have to occasionally take a big leap of faith, even if you can't see where you're going to land. I trusted Britney, she trusted me, and we both trusted God. That seemed like a pretty good plan to me.

Some people have no faith, and that's a terrible thing. Whether it's your love of family or your love of God that you cling to (in our case, it was both), everyone needs hope to hang on to. And that's what faith is: the knowledge that no matter how lost you feel, there's someone guiding you. No one is alone. ❁

"We all knew that God had big plans for Britney."—Margaret Smith, friend

*Before I go onstage to perform, I like to pray with my dancers. I get a lot of strength from that.*

*I know I am blessed. Not every girl gets to perform at the tree-lighting ceremony at Rockefeller Plaza! I just try to be grateful for all the good things that have happened to me in my life.*

# The Power of Prayer

I keep a prayer journal and I write in it every night. It has Scriptures in it, and you kind of add your own thoughts and feelings—just a few words you want to jot down. Sometimes I'll write about something that upset me that day or something that lifted my spirits.

I think my favorite saying is "Live each day to the fullest as if it were your last." I think that's so beautiful, and I've always let it guide me. You should soak up life, give everything you do your all, and cherish every moment, no matter how small. Life is so precious, and it scares me that people don't realize that until it's too late. If I need reminding of this, I just call Mama or Aunt Sandra. They're both people who know how to appreciate the simple things. There's nothing, for example, as good as a cold glass of iced tea on a hot summer day or the smell of fresh-cut grass in the backyard. I love when my little teacup poodle, Lady, rolls over and begs me to rub her tummy—it makes me smile just thinking about it. God created a beautiful world and sometimes we get so busy that we forget to notice all these wonders great and small. That's why I jot them down—so they stay with me.

I pray all the time. Every night before I go to sleep, I thank God for what I have and ask Him to watch over me and all the people I love. Right before we go onstage for a concert, we all join hands—all the dancers, all the musicians, all the crew—and I lead us in a prayer. I find a lot of comfort and strength in knowing I can talk to God and He's listening. That's the way we were raised, and my family still goes to church on Sundays. I don't think I could ever look at how lucky I am now and not think that God had a hand in it. ✿

# Life in a Small Town

My hometown is the kind of place where everyone knows everyone else—people honk their horns and yell "Hi, y'all!" when they pass you on the road. (Although Mama will tell you they're honking their horns at me because I'm a bad driver!) They'll stop you on the street to ask how you did on your geometry test. There's a real feeling of pride and kinship in our little town, and people look out for one another. I love everything about my home, except maybe for one little thing: everybody knows everybody else's business.

You can imagine what happened when I started going around and doing talent competitions and auditioning far away in big cities like New York: well, we were quite the buzz over at the City Cafe. Everyone had an opinion about it. Some even thought my family was crazy.

Other folks, however, thought it was great and really cheered me on—especially when I did finally get to be a Mouseketeer when I was eleven. (The second time must be the charm.) Practically the whole town turned out to send me and Mama off to Orlando, where the show was taped. They all had "Britney Spears Fan Club" T-shirts that they made up specially for me, and they had a huge cake. They even declared it the Official Britney Spears Day in Kentwood. Now, you know you wouldn't find that in a place like New York or L.A., but in a small town you're a family.

Today, my friends from Kentwood—Laura Lynne, Elizabeth, Jansen, Cortney, Wendy, Erin, and Cindy—are still my best friends in the world, and we make sure we stay in touch (writing, calling, visiting, you name it). These are the girls I was in day care and dance lessons with—we just go way back. I know a lot of people who lost touch with their friends when they got all wrapped up in show business. Well, that's like losing touch with who you are: I don't care how busy you are—you make time for the people who mean a lot to you. That goes for family, that goes for friends. It doesn't take but a minute to call up and say, "Hey, what y'all up to?" ❋

# Tuned In

I think Britney is singlehandedly responsible for the majority of Kentwood getting cable television! When she became a Mouseketeer, everyone wanted to watch her on TV, but we didn't get the Disney Channel. So everyone started ordering it up, and pretty soon almost every TV in Kentwood was tuned in to see Brit sing, dance, and act. People still talk about the time she belted out "I Feel for You" with Justin Timberlake. The local news did stories about her; *The Kentwood Ledger* and *The Hammond Daily Star* ran tons of articles. And outside our little town, Britney was becoming a national celebrity. When she walked around Walt Disney World in Orlando, fans would recognize her and ask for an autograph. It was very exciting, and also a little bit like a dream. Brit had wanted this for so long and had worked so hard to get to where she was, and now it was finally happening for her. ❈

*"Britney has inspired a whole town—not just little girls but grown-ups, too—to follow their dreams. They say, 'If she can do it, so can I.' She's made such a contribution, there's talk of putting up a sign in Kentwood:* **Home of Britney Spears.** *"*—Buddy Powell, owner of the Golden Corral restaurant

*Who knew back in 1994 that the kids who signed this* **Mickey Mouse Club** *script—Brit, Justin Timberlake, and Ryan Gosling—would end up being so successful today?*

Love + Laugh

**FINAL DRAFT**

**#717**

**6/06/94**

PEACE
AND
HARMONY,

LOVE
ALWAYS.
Justin Timberlake

God
Bless
- Britney
Spears

I still can't believe that Christina Aguilera and I have known each other since **The All-New Mickey Mouse Club** days. We had a lot of fun together doing the show.

Here I am hanging out with my fellow Mouseketeers—Justin Timberlake on the right (he's in NSYNC now) and Ryan Gosling on the left (you might know him as Young Hercules!).

# MMC Mates

I think the *Mickey Mouse Club* was where I first learned the importance of being a team player. I got a little taste of it when I played basketball back home for my elementary school, Parklane Academy. I was the point guard and had to pass the ball for others to shoot at the basket. But I guess I was too young then to see the value of being part of something that's bigger than just you.

At first I would be disappointed if other Mouseketeers got to sing a solo and I didn't, or if someone got to dance downstage and I had to be in the back. Then it kind of hit me one day: so what? We were all in this together, we were all contributing to produce a great show. Putting aside your ego for the good of the whole is a hard lesson to learn.

I was very close to a lot of the kids on the show, especially the younger ones who started when I did. Justin Timberlake, Christina Aguilera, and I were good friends, and still are. I used to really idolize Keri Russell. She was older and a great dancer, and I wished I had her beautiful long curly hair. Sometimes I'll bump into her now at an event and we'll be like, "Hey! You remember that time when we had to wear goofy outfits for Hall of Fame Day?" It's so cool that so many of us have gone on to be successful in our careers—look at Justin and J. C. with NSYNC, Christina Aguilera, or Keri on *Felicity*. It's amazing, and when people ask me why our gang has gone on to do such great things, I can't explain it. I guess our casting director on *MMC* was a great judge of talent.

Even today, *MMC* is kind of an extended family. We all stay in touch—even our mamas still talk—and I get a big kick every time I read that one of my fellow Mouseketeers is doing something great.

# Britney and Lynne Spears' Family Ties

Laura Lynne and I have been best friends since we we were born. In tutus and ballet slippers at our very first dance recital, I was the serious one on the right while she was just having a great time. (Even today, that girl knows how to make me laugh.) And aren't we such proper little ladies at age five in those frilly dresses and hair ribbons?

Over the years, there have been so many people—and not just kin—whom we've thought of as members of our family. We love and care about them (and they feel the same way about us). If you're lucky enough to have such special people in your life, always keep them close to you…and to your heart.

—Britney and Lynne

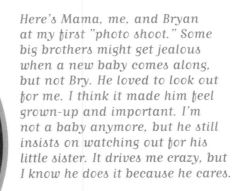

Here's Mama, me, and Bryan at my first "photo shoot." Some big brothers might get jealous when a new baby comes along, but not Bry. He loved to look out for me. I think it made him feel grown-up and important. I'm not a baby anymore, but he still insists on watching out for his little sister. It drives me crazy, but I know he does it because he cares.

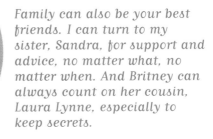

Family can also be your best friends. I can turn to my sister, Sandra, for support and advice, no matter what, no matter when. And Britney can always count on her cousin, Laura Lynne, especially to keep secrets.

We're all so proud of Britney. The whole Spears family (from left, her daddy, Jamie; me; little sister, Jamie Lynn; and big brother, Bryan) helped her celebrate at her platinum album party in New York.

When I was on the **All-New Mickey Mouse Club**, Laura Lynne and Jamie Lynn would hang out with me on the back lot at Walt Disney World. But I think Jamie Lynn was more interested in all those Disney characters walking around the park than in my show!

Laura Lynne is like a sister to me. Sometimes I just have to call her up to say "Hey" for no reason at all except to hear her voice—and of course, to get all the Kentwood gossip!

Everyone says my little sister, Jamie Lynn, is a "Mini-Me." She is the sweetest kid, and I just know she's going to be a big star herself one day.

Lounging with my fellow Mouseketeers, along with Laura Lynne and Jamie Lynn, in the wardrobe room. The show was so much fun (thanks to the people on it), it hardly felt like work at all. That's Justin Timberlake on the far right and Ryan Gosling on our laps!

When I became a Mouseketeer, all the kids on **MMC** became my family. Justin Timberlake and Ryan Gosling were some of my closest friends on the show. I am still close to J. C. and Justin; see them with me and Mama below.

You gotta have friends: When I was fifteen, my favorite thing to do was go to the mall in New Orleans with Cortney, Elizabeth, and Laura. Here we are celebrating the fact that I just got my braces off! I stay in touch with all of them today. Mama always told me everything changes in life, but friends are forever.

My girlfriends today just love to goof around. And as you can see from this picture, I'm chowing down with Cortney on the left, Laura Lynne and Jansen on the right.

Brit may have had her Mouseketeers, but Felicia Culotta, Jill Prescott, and I are the Three Musketeers. We've known one another for years, and I don't know what I'd do without either of them in my life.

When I started touring, I was homesick, so my gang on the road became my honorary family (and they still are today). All I have to do is look around me onstage to know that my dancers are behind me all the way—literally!

Those crazy NSYNC guys were all like my big brothers. I give them credit for showing me the ropes when it came to concerts. It also made it much easier, since I already knew Justin and J. C. from *MMC*. It was like a class reunion when we started touring together.

*At my eighteenth birthday party in New York City, all my family—the ones who are related to me and the ones who aren't—turned out for my big day. If I could make one wish on my birthday candles again, it would be that they'll all always be there to share good times with me.*

Brit's manager, Larry, has been like family to her. I know he loves her almost as much as Britney's daddy and I do!

*Like mother, like daughter: I love it when people say I'm just like my mama, because she is the finest person I know.*

# Stick With It

For kids, and even for grown-ups, it's always much easier to throw in the towel than to stick to your guns. You're tired, you're frustrated, things are not going exactly as you wanted (or not going at all). The heck with it, right? There were times when that child was so tired, I questioned if we shouldn't just forget about everything. After all, other kids aren't working at eleven. They are playing with Barbies or watching TV or playing video games. But as I've said, this was what Brit wanted. This was fun for her, even if it was work, and if that was the case, we were going to have the right attitude to get her as far as she could go. If Britney had gotten frustrated when things didn't go perfectly, we never would have gotten much farther than our own backyard. We Spearses can be stubborn when we need to be. You can't convince us otherwise when we believe in something strongly. People will try and sway you, or you may even talk yourself out of a goal. But Rome wasn't built in a day, and no dream is, either. If you want something bad enough, then give it time.

Most kids have a pretty short attention span. As a teacher, I can assure you of that! I look at Jamie Lynn and her friends and I just have to laugh: a few years ago, all she wanted to be when she grew up was Belle from *Beauty and the Beast*. Last year it was either an Olympic gymnast or Michael Jordan. Now she wants to be a singer, and next year—who knows! Maybe she'll want to be president! She changes her mind with the wind, which at a young age is fine. She should be free to fantasize about what the future will hold and let her curiosity run wild. But when you *do* know what you want in life (and with Brit, she knew right from the start), don't abandon it because your goal is harder to achieve than you anticipated. As a parent, you may also have to be a cheerleader for your child: "You can do it, I know you can! Hang in there!" It's much easier for kids to stand tall and strong if they have someone standing right by their side. ❊

*"I have never known someone so focused, so determined, as Britney. 'It can't be done' is not in her vocabulary."* —Larry Rudolph, manager

# The Zone

When I get into my dance mode, nothing in the world can get me out of it. One of my managers, Larry Rudolph (I have two managers, Larry and Johnny Wright), calls it "the Zone." As in, "Don't even try to talk to her now, she's in the Zone." I swear, Ben Affleck could walk right in (you know, I have the biggest crush on him), and I wouldn't notice. I will practice and practice a move in front of a mirror, over and over again—ten, twenty, a hundred times—until I'm happy with it. It needs to feel natural for me, not strained or awkward. It's something I've been doing since I was a little kid. I used to give myself dance report cards after a performance, grading myself on my execution. I think I probably still do that mentally nowadays: I'm my own toughest critic. But when I work really hard at it, when I tune out all the distractions and just focus, after practicing for a while, I begin to think, "You know, that's not so bad."

You can't ever expect to improve if you don't practice. And no one is so perfect (even a big star) that they couldn't stand some improvement. I don't like to do the same moves all the time the way some performers do. Each of my videos has a different look and new choreography, and I like that because it keeps me on my toes—literally! My dancers and I work real hard on learning those steps. The first day of rehearsals can be pretty funny, with all of us crashing into one another until we get it down. It's a lot of sweat and aches and pains, but the end result is this awesome production number that we're proud of. Sometimes I think, "Lordy, we are just never gonna get this thing to work right." But we keep plugging away, and before you know it, it's beat! ✿

*I work so hard on my routines with my dancers. I've been working hard since I was a little kid, and it sure has paid off!*

Okay, so I wasn't always a fashion plate. Get a load of this costume from a dance recital I did when I was little!

## Chapter 7
### Tackling the Tough Stuff

# Mirror, Mirror

I can remember being twelve or thirteen and hating the way I looked. I hated my hair (too thin); I hated my nose (too big); I hated my teeth (they stuck out funny and were crooked). I even hated my feet! I would look at Keri Russell when we were on *MMC*, and I'd want so badly to look and be like her. Now that I'm eighteen, there are days when I'm still not too thrilled with most of the above, although thanks to years of braces, I now love my smile. But I'm happy with the *whole* picture, and that's what's important. You can obsess over your negatives or you can emphasize your positives: maybe you have beautiful blue eyes, shiny long hair, or a great sense of humor. Every girl feels a little insecure sometimes. Even me. So what can you do about it?

Well, you can go and copy every new trend out there just to fit in with the crowd. But then you'll be spending a lot of money on some really tacky clothes. You can talk and act like the most popular girls in your school so they'll think you're cool, but that's lying to yourself as well as everyone else. Or you can hide in your room, hoping this phase will eventually pass. At some point you're going to realize, just as I did, that the only person you need to please is you. I'm not saying this self-confidence hit me overnight exactly. (I do recall perming my hair in high school because everyone else did, and I couldn't wait for it to grow out!) Now, though, I don't worry so much about what people think. I dress the way I want to dress; I don't pretend to be someone I'm not. I express myself in ways that make me feel good about myself. That's what fashion should be about.

And as for hating what you see when you look in the mirror, that will pass, I promise. My tin grin didn't last forever, though it seemed like it would at the time. And when I run into Keri now, I don't think about how I want to be as pretty and poised as she is, I just think about how nice it is to see her. You aren't alone—most kids feel like ugly ducklings at some time or another. But remember, you have something special and wonderful that is uniquely your own. Sometimes you just have to look a little deeper to find it. ❁

"Britney is so beautiful—on the inside as well as the outside."—Sandra Covington, aunt

I am much more confident about how I dress now than I was when I was younger. You just have to follow your own style.

# Be True to You

When Brit came home after three seasons on the *Mickey Mouse Club*, she told us she just wanted to be a regular kid for a year: she wanted to go to school, homecoming, the prom. But it didn't take very long for her to realize that she missed performing. She was bored, and her father and I could see how unhappy she was. I think it was a very difficult time for her, a time when she really had to give some serious thought to what she wanted to do with her life. That's a hard enough decision for a grown-up to make, much less a fifteen-year-old. She really had everything going for her at school—she was getting good grades, her classmates voted her Most Beautiful in the yearbook. But as hard as she tried to fit into life in Kentwood once again, it wasn't where her heart was.

I think she was frustrated here. It was such a comedown for her: no challenge. She'd been in the adult working world, and in high school there was all this silliness and pettiness. You know how some teenage girls can be: it was all about popularity and being in the right group. Well, she just hated that. She couldn't understand why everyone wasn't treated equally, why a jock couldn't be friends with someone on the chess team. Now, what would be wrong with that? She was always nice to everyone and she hated people who were backstabbing or judgmental. ❁

*Mouseketeers together again. Brit is hanging out here with her friends Justin and J. C. from NSYNC.*

# Style File

People are constantly asking me, "Britney, did you always know what your look was going to be?" And they want to copy my clothes and accessories and hair. What's my look? I'm not even sure yet, because I like dressing in lots of different outfits and trying new styles all the time. The crop tops and hiphuggers I wore in some of my videos were the kind of clothes we used to wear in Kentwood (it can be scorching during the summer, so the barer the better!), and I'm real comfortable dancing in them. But I love to experiment with clothes and makeup and hair—I'm such a girl! I don't think it's a good idea to ever get too set in your ways—or worse, to become a slave to the trends. You should set your own trends.

I admire the way Madonna always reinvents herself. I think that's one reason she's managed to stay a success for so long while other artists have fizzled out. She's always got a few surprises up her sleeve. I've tried a lot of hairstyles these past two years—long with extensions, bangs, no bangs; then I got it cut it to shoulder length. I think it's okay if your style keeps evolving; you should keep evolving, too. Can you just imagine how silly I would look if I dressed the same at forty as I do now?

Rather than inspiring teenage girls to copy me, I hope I inspire them to do their own thing. Be bold, be creative, be different, be expressive—and be proud of who you are. ✳

# Dress Stress

I'm all for individuality and creativity in fashion, but I would not be honest if I told you I approved of every outfit Britney has wanted to wear. And I'm not just talking about now. Even when she was in high school, she and her girlfriends used to wear some of those crazy trends that went in and out. But I don't see any real harm in it, and I don't believe that makes me a bad mother, either. People have criticized Britney for dressing a little too sexy for her age. Well, this is what I have to say to that: She dresses appropriately for where she's at and the business she's in. She's a pop singer. If she's at a glitzy awards show, then she should look a little "rock-n-roll." If she's on the cover of a music magazine, then what's wrong with wearing something flashy and fun? They are costumes; she does not dress this way every day. She knows just how far to go with her fashion and what I will and won't like. (She likes to be an individual, but she also wants her mama's blessing.) Sometimes she'll hold up something outrageous and smile and say, "Mama, do you think this is too sexy?" Well, she already knows my answer ("Britney, that is just *too* much!") and she'll put it back on the rack. And if I'm not there, then Larry, her manager, or her friend Fe are the ones in charge, and let me tell you, sometimes they're more conservative than I am!

*I was so happy that my first tour was with NSYNC, because I've known these guys for such a long time. Here I am with Lance.*

Look, I don't love her belly-button ring. (I said, "Britney, why did you go and do that to yourself?" and she said, "But Mama, it's real cute!") Nor do I understand tattoos (fake or real ones). You show me a mama who does! But Britney is eighteen now. I can't be dressing her in those frilly dresses and Mary Janes the way I did when she was nine. She's becoming a woman, and she's trying to look more grown-up. I can't hold that against her. But what I have always insisted upon is that she dress appropriately for where she is going. If she ever tried to go to church in beaded leather pants, I wouldn't let her out the door! But Brit would never do that. She knows what's right and wrong. If we ever disagree on her clothes, then we talk about it. Talk, not argue. If you threaten your teenager ("You are *not* wearing that!"), then you know she's going to do it anyway just to spite you. Try compromising, try reasoning, and then remember to keep it in perspective. Is dying her hair bright pink the end of the world? It will grow out. Is that itty-bitty miniskirt so unreasonable for a Saturday night dance? At least she's not wearing it to the supermarket.

Britney and I respect each other's tastes and opinions. I think most of the time her clothes are just beautiful. (If I were her age and had her figure, I'd wear them myself.) And as for her belly-baring crop tops that everyone was making such as issue out of, well, I have to laugh, because that's my influence. When I worked at the health club, I was always working out in those little athletic tops, so she's just copying her mama. ✿

# An Open-Door Policy

I feel that I can tell my mama anything and she won't overreact or sit in judgment. Instead, she'll sit and listen, no matter what hour of the morning or night (I have this knack for calling her at 1 A.M.). It's always been that way between us—I know Jamie Lynn and Bryan feel the same way. Of course, sometimes when I was growing up it was a little embarrassing talking about boys and stuff, but she always made it easy. I could always tell when it was time for a serious talk, because she'd go, "Now, Britney…" She was also good at making me feel I wasn't the only one who went through these things. She used to tell me all these stories about when she was a teenager (you know, she hated her hair, too?) and how Aunt Sandra used to have to fill her in on everything because her mama was shy about it. Well, I was lucky my mama wasn't shy—because my older sibling, Bryan, was just as protective as Daddy, and if it had been up to him I would never have had a date! ❁

# Words of Wisdom

There is no easy way to talk to your children about sex or drugs or alcohol. But you have to do it some time—sooner rather than later—because you want them to be safe. Spiritually, I know what God means for sex, and I think you should wait till after you're married. But, times being what they are, it's unrealistic for me to close my eyes and refuse to see that there are a lot of kids out there who are active. I wanted my children to be aware of what it means (it's a beautiful thing and should be out of love, not just lust) and what the risks are. I want them to understand how dangerous it is to take drugs or to drink and drive. When your babies go off to college, you don't know what they're being exposed to. And I don't know what Brit is seeing when she's off working. She's traveling all over the world, and it's hard to keep track of what city she's in, let alone whether she's causing trouble anywhere! But I know I have prepared her; I have told her how I feel, and I trust that she will make smart decisions. That's all a parent can do. You can't live your child's life for her.

When it comes to these tough talks, don't laugh, don't belittle their curiosity or innocence. Look your child straight in the eyes and address every question with respect and dignity. If you make it comfortable for her to talk to you, she will. I think I had a lot of practice before my own kids were of that age because all the neighbors' teenagers used to come over to our house. I was always counseling, helping with term papers, so I was like an honorary mom. I guess it was less stressful to talk to me than to their own parents.

Brit celebrated her seventeenth birthday on the tour bus. Even if I can't be with her all the time, she knows I'm just a phone call away. (And we sure spend a lot of time on the phone!)

When Britney's on the road, I have to trust that she's in good hands. I know she gets along with her dancers just fine. Here she is with T.J., on the far right, and a friend—this picture is from their first tour. (That first tour was the hardest for me!)

You also can't worry yourself sick everytime your teenager goes out on a date and you're not there to watch her. With Brit, I was lucky. I never worried because I knew every boy in Kentwood. Not only that, but I knew every boy's daddy and his granddaddy. She was fourteen when she started going out to proms and homecoming dances and fifteen before she dated once a week. The only arguments we ever had were about her steady boyfriend practically living in our house. That boy just never wanted to go home! He was always in front of our TV with his feet up on the couch. But we worked it out: I explained to Britney that she needed to spend some more time with her family and other people, and not just her beau. It was either that or I was going to have to start charging him rent!

Growing up, she had her curfews to keep to, and she seldom broke them. She still has a curfew when she's home today. I can't control what she does on the road, but when she's under my roof I want to know that she's safe. Both Brit and Bryan have always respected my wishes, and they've always confided in me. Bry's now engaged and will be getting married to a lovely girl, Blaize, whom I just love. (Everyone says Bry picked a girl who looks just like his mama!) And Britney has no problem gossiping with her mama about boys. We don't deal much right now with the dating issues, because with her work she barely has time to sleep, much less date. But when the time comes and she needs me, I'm here. There's nothing we can't get through if we put our heads together. ❊

*It's hard to be a mama sometimes when your daughter is running all over the world. But sometimes I do get to travel with her. (And I love to travel!) Brit and I are in Singapore here for a show she did for her record label before "...Baby One More Time" came out.*

"My first impression of Brit when she was little was 'cute kid.' Then I saw her on stage. How on earth did such a big voice come out of such a little person? Today, she's like my little sister and we're so tight. I'm lucky enough to know her better than most: I know that she can't get into an elevator without singing in it (great acoustics, she insists). She gets that from her mama, because Lynne will sing anytime, anywhere. Although she doesn't quite have Brit's talent, I tell her she makes a joyful noise unto the Lord."—Felicia Culotta, chaperone

# With a Little Help from Our Friends

Everyone needs a shoulder to lean on. Brit and I have each other, but we also have a great group of loving friends and family members. We call them our dream team because they helped us make Brit's dreams come true. We turn to them when we have fears, doubts, dilemmas—or just when we need a little pep talk. Britney has created this incredible group around her in her professional life: her managers and representatives, her bodyguard and guardian, her dancers and crew. There isn't one of them she wouldn't hesitate to call on in time of need, and they'd do anything in the world for her.

But it's not only stars who need a support system. Everyone could use one: maybe your girlfriends at the office or your bunkmates at camp or your neighbors down the street. Whoever they are, they should make you feel comfortable and confident. They're the folks who'd never complain if you called them at 2 A.M. in a panic.

It's so important to surround yourself with people whom you trust. You don't want to be worrying about what their motives are when you find yourself in a rough spot. Because Brit was just a teenager when she started recording "Baby" and when the album came out, it was even more important to find people who would not only help advance her career but also watch over her.

We recruited the first member of Britney's team shortly after she decided she wanted to leave Kentwood and get back into the business after *Mickey Mouse Club* had ended. I remember we had another one of our little family discussions and decided, "Okay, let's see where we can get if we focus on her singing." Sure enough, along came an offer for her to join an all-girl singing group, Innosense. It was exciting, but it presented a problem. We weren't quite sure it was the best choice for her—she had always envisioned herself as a solo singer, not as part of a group. Again we had the pros and cons to weigh, and this time we needed a little help.

Over the past few years, we'd stayed in touch with an entertainment lawyer in New York City, Larry Rudolph. He had met Brit when she was thirteen. At the time, her father and I took her to his office and she barely said a word. Larry told us the time wasn't right for a young pop singer: pop wasn't what was selling (hip-hop was), and he was convinced that if we just waited, tastes in music would change again.

Now we called Larry to ask his opinion on her joining Innosense. We had two weeks to let the group's managers know. Larry listened, and this time he sounded a little more optimistic. The Backstreet Boys were huge, Hanson was hot, but what the music industry was lacking was a female teenage artist. He didn't want to let on at the time, but he had a hunch that Britney's big break was about to happen and that solo was the way to go.

*"Stars all have this certain inexplicable quality about them—it's hard to put a finger on it, but I knew Britney had it. When she was thirteen, I thought she was sweet, but at fifteen, when I saw her pictures (she was the most beautiful girl any record label could hope for) and heard her voice on tape, I was convinced she was the real thing."*—Larry Rudolph, manager

*Here is Brit with one of her managers, Johnny Wright. She trusts him completely—and so do I!*

# Laying the Tracks

I can totally understand why Larry had no idea what to advise us. A lot can change between the ages of thirteen and fifteen. What if I looked like a goob and my voice had changed? At least he was honest about it, which is what I love most about Larry. He'll tell you exactly what he's thinking, no beating around the bush.

So he asked us to send him some current pictures and a demo tape. A demo tape? Was he kidding? I didn't have anything like that. Do you know how expensive those are to make? But he said it didn't matter what kind of recording I sent. He told my mom just to hold a tape recorder and let me sing into it. So we made a recording and shipped it off to Larry.

By some small miracle, he liked what he saw and heard. He told me he would shop me around to some record labels, but first I needed a real demo. We didn't have any money to hire studio musicians, and we certainly didn't have the time—the clock was ticking. So Larry called in a favor: he asked a record producer he represented to send him a tape of a song that had just been cut from an album he was working on with Toni Braxton. It was called "Today," and they had thought it was "too pop" for Toni (but Larry thought it was perfect for me). So he sent us two versions of the song—one with just the instrumentals and one with Toni singing along. So I learned the song by copying the way she sang it.

We went into a local studio in Louisiana and recorded my vocals over the music tracks. Then Larry flew me into New York City on a Thursday morning and we went to six different offices that day—two music publishers and four labels. At each office, I would have to sing (to some karaoke tapes, because that was pretty much all I had) and answer questions for a bunch of top record executives. Lordy, I have never been more nervous in my whole life! I've always said that I can sing in front of a crowd of fifty thousand and I'm fine, but put me in a room with four people staring right at me and I'm a wreck! If you ask Larry, he'll tell you he's not sure who was more nervous—me or him. He stood right by me that whole time, assuring me I could do it.

I went home that night totally spent, but I knew I had given it my best shot. I remember looking out the airplane window, as we soared into the clouds, and wondering what the next two weeks held in store. ✿

# Waiting for an Answer

We were biting our nails until Larry called us with the news: two of the labels had turned Britney down, one was on the fence, and JIVE still had yet to respond. But Larry was very hopeful. Clive Calder, JIVE's president, was very smart, and he would surely "get" Britney's potential appeal. Well, he was right: Clive wanted to give Brit a contract—but with one small stipulation. He wanted a ninety-day "out clause." That way, if he didn't like what Brit was doing in the studio, the label had the option to take back the contract. Well, it wasn't exactly a vote of confidence, but we were thrilled nonetheless. Besides, it wasn't the first time Britney'd had to prove herself. We all knew she'd wow them, and we were right—after only a month, Clive called Larry and said Britney was great, even more wonderful than he had expected, and he was sure the album would be a huge hit. ❉

# A Friend in Fe

Once we signed the contracts, JIVE set me up with two great producers: Eric Foster White in New Jersey (he had worked with Whitney Houston) and Max Martin in Stockholm, Sweden (he had produced albums by the Backstreet Boys, Ace of Base, and Robyn). So I'd be doing quite a bit of traveling to both places, and that meant being away from home. Mama had her job teaching second grade and Jamie Lynn, who was only about five, to take care of. Clearly I needed someone to be with me on my big adventure.

Enter Felicia Culotta. I call her Fe, and so does practically everyone else, because it just suits her better. She's my guardian and goes with me everywhere, but I really think of her more as a big sister. We go way back: she used to be a pediatric dental hygienist, just like my mama's girlfriend Jill, and it was Jill who introduced us. I was probably about eight years old, and I was booked to sing at an arts-and-crafts festival that was running on Oak Alley, a beautiful Louisiana plantation that Jill's sister managed. Anyway, Fe came along for the ride that weekend—she and I were in the backseat of the car, and Mama and Jill were up front chatting away. She was nice and all, but I was shy and didn't say much, so it was a long ride for both of us. When we got to the festival, there were so many amazing things to buy: candles and comforters and crocheted sweaters, beautiful glassware and carved wood. I, however, had my eye on a stand of cute baby dolls, and Mama promised she'd buy me one after my performance (I got $50 and food coupons as pay for my performance).

*I was so lucky to be working with Eric Foster White on "...Baby One More Time." He's such a great producer, and a real nice guy as well. (His wife, Karin, is the best, too.) I really want to learn how to play guitar, and he was helping me pick around when this picture was taken.*

*"From the first time I met Britney, I saw this was a person whom everyone can like. I knew she'd become a hit around the world."*

—Max Martin, producer

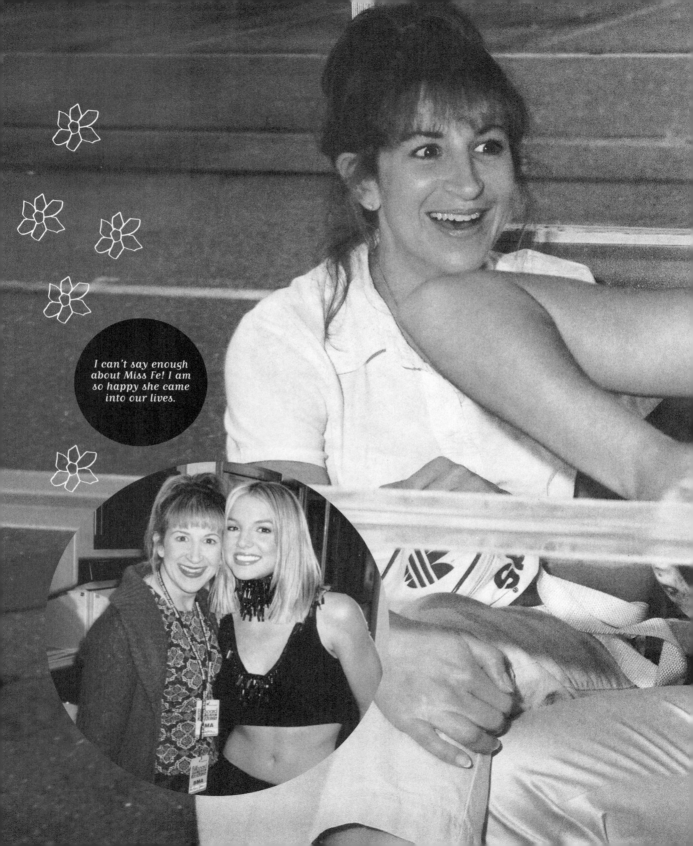

I can't say enough about Miss Fe! I am so happy she came into our lives.

Fe and Brit are goofing off here, but I know I can count on Fe to take care of my baby.

Mama prepared me as she always did, taking her lipstick out of her purse and dabbing it on my lips and cheeks. (It made me feel so glamorous!) I looked pretty good, if I do say so myself—but I was missing the finishing touch: a pair of earrings. Mama had forgotten hers, so Fe quickly whipped hers off and gave them to me. They were these big silver hoops, and I just loved them.

I got up there onstage and started to sing, and pretty soon a crowd began to gather. Before long the grass in front of the stage was filled with hundreds of people and I was having a ball. Fe was right up front with Jill and Mama, and she had this amazed look on her face. After I took my bows, I jumped offstage and grabbed Fe by the hand and dragged her off to go buy a doll with me. That was when we became friends for the first time.

The next time was about seven years later. Fe had stayed in touch with Mama—they would catch up mainly over Christmas—and eventually she moved out of Louisiana to become a nanny in Westchester, New York. She had decided to leave that job and was looking for another one when Mama gave her a ring and said we were in New York. Did she want to have dinner with us? Well, over dinner, Mama laid her cards on the table. She said she had an ulterior motive for the invitation. I was about to embark on recording my first album, and she needed someone to sort of act as my chaperone. Mama said it would make her feel so much better to know that a friend of the family was watching over me, but she didn't want to steal Fe away from the family she was working for. (She had no idea that Fe had just quit her job!) Fe thought about it—maybe she figured she needed a paycheck anyway—and said yes to looking after me for three months. Mama promised her that I was hardly any trouble at all, but I'm not so sure Fe believed her or loved the idea of chasing a teenager around the world. I wasn't too thrilled about it, either—we didn't know each other that well anymore at that point, and I wasn't sure what to think of this thirty-two-year-old nanny. The last thing a fifteen-year-old wants is a baby-sitter cramping her style!

*Miss Felicia and me in the "Baby" video.*

Luckily, we hit it off instantly—probably because Fe is so cool to be around. She has been with me every step of the way. She doesn't like to be called my guardian or my chaperone (I think it makes her feel too grown-up and serious), so I just say, "Fe takes care of me." And she does, whether it's making sure I eat my breakfast in the morning (eggs Benedict, she knows, is my absolute favorite) or hustling me off to the studio because I'm late (she's big on yelling "Five minutes! Five minutes!") or snapping photos for my scrapbook (you'd be amazed at the great shots this woman can take with a disposable camera!). I feel like she's my right arm, and I don't know what I'd do without her in my life. You know the teacher in my "…Baby One More Time" video? Well, that's Miss Felicia in costume. (She doesn't wear those nerdy glasses in real life, I promise you!) I just had to give her a chance to be a star, too.

We're glad we found each other, not just once but twice. Fe made those first crazy days of making my album so much more fun and less scary. ✿

*"For her eighteenth birthday, her record company gave her a diamond necklace, and she couldn't believe how beautiful it was. She said, 'Look at this, Miss Margaret, is this not fine? And it's mine!' Then she said I could borrow it anytime I want. She's amazing. Anything that girl has, she's willing to share with the people she loves."* —Margaret Smith, friend

# A Surrogate Mama

There was no other way of making this work. Brit needed to be moving around, and I couldn't uproot Jamie Lynn for a year. Besides my own child, there were several others back at Springcreek Elementary who counted on me to teach their class, and Britney's daddy had to work as well. No mother wants to have someone taking her place, so of course I wasn't 100 percent sure about letting Fe step in as Britney's guardian. Giving your child to someone else's care is a very hard thing. Just think of how many lists most parents leave for a baby-sitter when they're just going out to dinner at night. Well, I was leaving Brit for several months, so you can just imagine the mile-long list I gave poor Fe! I told her that her most important job—more than watching out for Brit—was to make sure she helped her keep a good attitude. I must have said that to her 50 million times! In the past, I had always been there to cheer my baby on—even if she dropped her little hat in the middle of a dance number, she could see me out front in the audience giving her the thumbs-up. I needed Fe to be Britney's cheerleader from now on. And she does a great job in that department, always making her feel good about herself and her work.

So I put my trust in Fe and she turned out to be one of our greatest blessings. Not only does she take care of Brit, but she takes care of me, too! Sometimes if Brit's busy in the studio and can't get to a phone, she'll just call me and say, "Now, Lynne, don't you worry. She's doing just fine." Every time I do start to worry, I remind myself that Fe loves her and protects her as if she were her own. You always pray that your child has an angel watching over her: we were lucky that our angel happened to be looking for a new job. 🌸

*This was a hard moment for me. I was sending Britney off with Fe for her first concert. I got a little emotional at the airport, but it was easy to see that Brit and Fe were going to get along just fine.*

# Putting It Together

Fe and I headed first to New Jersey to work with Eric Foster White. He was so wonderful to me and really showed me the ropes when it came to recording. He also taught me how to play darts (I'm pretty good now). You know that line in "From the Bottom of My Broken Heart" that says, "You drove a dart straight through my heart?" Well, we got inspired! Fe also was an inspiration: Eric wrote "E-mail My Heart" after he taught her how to e-mail her boyfriend on the computer.

I got real close to him and his wife, Karin, and they made me feel like family when I was missing mine something fierce. I've been lucky that way with all of the people I work with—they kind of adopt me as an honorary family member. I've spent Thanksgiving with my manager Larry and his family, and several birthdays on the road with my dancers. Mama always told me that family is the most important thing in your life, so I'm lucky I have all these different families in mine. You don't have to be kin to care about one another.

*Larry Rudolph, the man on the right, is the best manager I could have found. He not only helps my career, but he's a good friend, too. He and I are with superproducer Max Martin (he's the one who made "Baby" sound so great) at the MTV Video Music Awards.*

My next family—one that I spent almost a year with—spoke another language entirely. Sweden, the second stop on my recording schedule, was my first trip abroad, and I was both excited and scared. The plane ride over didn't help matters, either. The turbulence was the worst I have ever experienced. I remember I got up to go to the bathroom, and when I came back the plane was bouncing so bad I couldn't make it back to my seat. I started to cry, and Fe couldn't get to me—the flight attendants wouldn't let her unbuckle her seat belt. Eventually, I managed to get seated, and for the rest of the trip I was white-knuckled and doing a lot of praying. When we landed, I announced that I never wanted to get on an airplane again. Poor Fe had visions of us taking a boat back to the United States! Luckily, I changed my mind a little later when I calmed down, but I still hate to fly.

Stockholm is a beautiful city, but I didn't get to see very much of it. Most days, we were recording from 2 P.M. till 2 A.M., with maybe an hour break for dinner around 7:00. I'm not much of a morning person—my voice doesn't wake up till about noon, so these were the hours that worked best for us. Max Martin was amazing, and so were all of the musicians. They were such fun guys—all Swedish—and they made me feel so at home. It took about a year for us to wrap the whole thing; I had my sweet sixteen right in the middle. Some of the songs were pop—the kind that just make you feel good and make you want to party. Others, like "From the Bottom of My Broken Heart," which I did with Eric, were really soulful. Most of them were about love and relationships. I'd only had one serious boyfriend in school for two years, so I hadn't really experienced all the emotions I had to sing about. But Max made me feel very secure and showed me some cool techniques for my voice. As I began to relax, I added a little of my own style and attitude.

I think the song that blew me away the first minute I heard it was "...Baby One More Time." We had been working on the album for about six months, and Max played it for me. In a word, it was...*wow*. He felt the same way, and we decided it would be the first single we'd release. I will never forget the date it hit the stores: October 23, 1998. I'm so lucky to work with Max, because of his incredible instinct—he knows not only what will make a great song but also what I will love singing. ✤

# This Is the Moment

It still takes my breath away when I think about the first time I heard one of Britney's songs on the radio. I was in the gym, and thank God my girlfriend Jill was there. Remember that shoulder to lean on I said you sometimes need? Well, if ever I needed one, it was then. I could not stop crying (I was making quite the scene) and I made Jill cry, too. We cried together—all day. I can't begin to explain what I felt: relief, joy, gratitude (luckily, Jill didn't need me to explain it to her). That was my baby on the radio, singing the way she always said she'd do, and everything we had done as a family to make it happen, well, it all was worth it for that one incredible moment. I think I told everyone I knew. My phone didn't stop ringing all night with people calling to congratulate us. ✿

# Name That Tune

I was coming back to Kentwood after a long trip and I had just climbed into the back of my mama's car when I heard the first five notes on the radio. I let out such a scream! I thought it had to be fate, because that song came on the very minute we got in the car. But it wasn't fate—it was Mama. She had spent all morning calling the radio station, 104.1 in New Orleans, asking them to play it just around the time I was arriving. I could not believe it was my voice on the radio, that my song was already getting airtime. I think I rolled down the windows and cranked it up as loud as it would go so everyone in the airport garage could hear it. I was totally freaking. But that was only the beginning.

I got to perform in malls—JIVE thought it was very important to get my name and my music out there—and I toured as an opening act for NSYNC (pretty cool, because I'm good friends with Justin and J. C. from our *MMC* days). At first the girls in the audiences were not exactly psyched when I came onstage. They were too busy screaming for the guys: "I love you!" But after a while I won them over. The tour wasn't easy—we were always on the bus and I was homesick a lot, but all along I was learning and growing as a performer. And the guys in the the group, the crew, my dancers—they were all so awesome and we had some great times. ✿

# A New Attitude

Having supporting players in your life doesn't make you a weaker person. In fact, it builds up your confidence so you can be stronger and more independent. I see this in Britney; she's bolder and much more self-assured because she knows we're behind her. She called me when they told her what they were envisioning for her first video. They wanted "...Baby One More Time" to be a cartoonish space-rangers kind of thing. She said, "Mama, if I do that, I'm gonna look like such a fool!" So I told her to speak up, say what she thought the video should be about. She did just that, and Nigel Dicks, the director, thought it was brilliant. Brit suggested a group of kids waiting impatiently for the school bell to ring—and the rest is history (not to mention a great video).

She's no longer afraid to speak up. Why? Because Britney knows herself, she knows her audience, and most important, she knows there are a whole lot of people who believe in her. And because she trusts all these people in her life, including Fe and her managers, Larry and Johnny, and her producer Max, she knows that they won't let her fall or fail, but will work with her and help her grow as a performer and artist, and as a person. ✿

Britney has so many
young fans. She loves
all of them because
she remembers what
it's like to be a fan,
too. You should have
seen her when she met
Mariah Carey and
Whitney Houston!

# Living Large

Sometimes I have to pinch myself when I wake up in the morning to make sure I'm not dreaming all of this. I hoped and I prayed for this to happen, but you know, you're never *sure* it will. You think maybe you'll get some of what you want, that maybe hard work will pay off a little, but I never ever saw this coming! This is beyond anything we ever could have imagined. Sometimes it makes me laugh out loud because I'm so happy; other times, it makes me real quiet because I'm thinking about how lucky and blessed I am. I'll say, "Mama, can you believe it?" And she'll say, "Why, of course I can!" Then we'll both scream like crazy together.

I'm so lucky. I get to do exactly what I love to do, each and every day—and they pay me for it! There have been so many "best parts" to my success. But there are also a few things I don't love about it. Mama always tells me to every up there's a down; to every good there's a bad. And is that really so bad? I don't think so. I think you appreciate the high points in life more if you realize there are low ones, too. It gives you perspective.

For me, most of what I do is the ultimate. There is no feeling in the world like looking out into an audience and hearing them singing along with you—they know all the words to your songs. That's a kick, because you know you've touched them. Little girls are saving their allowances to buy my CD, the way I used to save mine to buy the new Madonna. That is such an amazing feeling.

Sometimes kids will come up to me and say, "Britney, I want to be just like you!" That is really sweet and flattering, but I certainly didn't ever think I'd wind up being called a role model. If I am, then I'm proud to be one, but I'm not doing anything different with my life because kids are looking up to me. I'm not acting any more responsibly—I'm hardly the type to rebel or go wild and crazy anyway. This is who I am, and if they can relate to me, that's great. I'm honored. But I don't want kids to idolize me or anything. I'm just a regular person, and I probably was a lot like them not too long ago. It's so hard for me to see my face on T-shirts and calendars and stuff because it's like, "Hey, y'all: that is me! It's not like it's Brad Pitt or something!" I call one of the Britney dolls that looks nothing like me "Monster Britney," and Fe and I crack up over it.

Another great part of my job is the traveling—all the people and places I have gotten to see: London, Paris, Japan, Sweden. Photo shoots are fun, too: I get to dress up in cool clothes and get my hair and makeup all glam. Laura Lynne and I used to love dressing up and smudging lipstick all over our faces when we were little, so things haven't changed all that much!

It has also been the biggest thrill going to the awards shows. I love the recognition—don't get me wrong—but even more fun than accepting an award has been getting to meet my childhood idols face-to-face. I positively *freak* when I see them backstage or I'm in the audience sitting next to them. At the MTV Europe Awards, I was like, "Mariah, I think you're so amazing!" and "Whitney, girl, you look good!" I made them take pictures with me. You know it!

*Here I am giving an award to NSYNC. I get a little nervous on these awards shows, but it was fun to be on stage again with my friends.*

I had to prove I was actually standing in the same room with these legendary divas. I felt like some crazed NSYNC fan around them. I was totally babbling because I was nervous. So much for Miss Sophisticated Star, huh? Anytime I hear someone has met someone famous, I just want to know: "What are they like? Are they so nice?" Everyone I've met so far in the music business has been great. If you had told me ten years ago that I was one day going to be hangin' with Mariah, I would have called you crazy! I did this tribute to Cher at the World Music Awards (I sang "The Beat Goes On" in a long black wig) and she came up to me afterward and said, "I love you, girl!" Can you believe Cher is telling little ol' me she likes my singing? Lordy, that is just too strange! But here I am, and I just have to wonder sometimes, "What did I ever do to deserve all this?" ✤

Someone pinch me—it's me with *Ricky Martin* and *Celine Dion!*

# Meet and Greet

She tries not to be starstruck—she works real hard at it. But sometimes Britney just can't help getting a little giggly. When she was with Whitney and Mariah, you could have knocked her over with a feather. What's so funny is that when fans are like that around her, all excited and nervous, she just looks at me and goes, "I don't get it—it's just me." She can't even imagine herself a star. I think we both have a tough time with that one. You just never think that anything this wonderful could happen to you. Other people maybe, other people with more money or more connections, but never you. That's why I think Brit is such an inspiration to kids, because she was just a regular little girl living in a small town in the middle of nowhere and she's come so far and done so much at such a young age. There are Britney dolls and posters, magnets, T-shirts—you name it. And to her it's no big deal. She forgets that she used to wallpaper her bedroom with her favorite stars' posters when she was little. I think she'd faint if she met Tom Cruise.

I'll admit I was a little giddy myself at the prospect of meeting royalty. Prince William is a big fan of Brit's and we were invited to meet him in London. My girlfriends and I couldn't stop squealing: can you imagine being asked to Buckingham Palace? When we got there, unfortunately, the timing was bad—the prince had been on a foxhunt all day and couldn't make it. But he and Britney have exchanged letters since—although if you believe what you read in the tabloids, they're practically engaged. We just laugh that one off because it couldn't be more wrong. Where do they get this stuff?

# Home Is Where Your Heart Is

I can't lie and say that there aren't some drawbacks to celebrity. Yes, I love the travel, but I hate that it takes me so far away from the people I love. Lately, I've been missing my little sister, Jamie Lynn, a whole lot. She's growing up and going through all those girl things, and I wish I could be there for her. Even just for the everyday stuff. She's taking gymnastics and I want to help her out with her handsprings. And I would have liked to be there more for Aunt Sandra, especially when she was going through her surgery and chemotherapy. But everyone understands. This is what I'm supposed to be doing, and we work it out. I fly my mama in to see me sometimes, and every six weeks I go home. When I tour this summer, I'm going to have every weekend off so I'll be able to see my family and friends much more. Kentwood is my home and it's where my heart is. I know that sounds corny, but it's where I'm happiest and where I can be totally myself. Of course, we have to keep it a secret now when I go back so we don't have 9 million people showing up at our front door. (Although if I left it up to Mama, she'd be inviting them all in for coffee.) ❀

# Across the Miles

It's so hard when Britney's away. I stay really, really busy and we talk to each other every day on the phone. It's not that I worry about her—I know good people are with her and keeping an eye on her—but I miss having her in my life every day. I miss her little laugh (she will crack up at any joke, I swear, even if she doesn't get it!) and seeing her with her hair swept up in a messy ponytail when she wakes up in the morning. I miss us snuggling on the couch together and having girl talk over coffee. Every time I walk by her bedroom and I see her doll collection, I get this little pang: gosh, I wish she was still a little girl and I could hold her in my arms or bounce her on my lap! It's funny—most moms don't have to deal with separation until their kids go off to college. With Brit, I've had to cope with being away from her so many times. I cry every time I have to put her on the plane. I can't help it—it never seems to get easier. Your baby is your baby, no matter how old she gets—or even if she has babies of her own. But I have to let her follow her dreams wherever they may take her, even if it's a world away from me. If you truly love someone, you have to give them the wings to fly. ❀

# The Party Scene

I am so *not* the party animal that it's kind of embarrassing. People are like, "Hey, Brit, come hang out with us," and I say, "Thanks, y'all, but no thanks. I'd much rather take a hot bubble bath and get a good night's sleep." I need my sleep—Fe has to practically drag me out of bed by noon because I'm so tired from working all day. I'm out cold the minute my head hits the pillow.

I don't really love the scene, anyway. Sometimes it makes me feel uncomfortable. I've been in a couple of clubs where people are drinking a lot and doing drugs and I'm like, "Get me out of here!" I don't understand that behavior—it's just so uncalled for.

It makes it all the more strange when the tabloids report that I was here or there, dating someone I never met. It's so crazy, because I rarely get out anywhere. And who has time to date all these guys they have me linked to? I don't pay very much attention to what they print anymore because most of it isn't true, but I know it hurts and worries my family and friends—especially my mom. She takes it personally. I just say, "Sticks and stones…" except when they write something that I think could be harmful. There are lots of girls who look up to me, and I would hate for them to do something that could hurt them because they thought I was doing it. I wish the tabloids could be a little bit more responsible and consider that what they print could have consequences. ❖

# Cruel Intentions

It tears me to pieces when people pick on Britney. I'm so close to my daughter, and I feel what she feels, so I can tell you that sometimes she really hurts. What I can't understand is why they do it, why people make up nasty stories that aren't true and criticize her. Sometimes I think that people are jealous of success and they feel the need to knock others down a few notches when they get too big. But what they forget is that Britney Spears is not just a performer, she's a person, too, with feelings. And even more than that. She's just a kid, so sensitive and vulnerable and in need of approval and affection, just like any other child. When a tabloid story comes out, it can feel like the whole world is against you. But we've learned the hard way that the more you deny it, the more attention you bring to it. Sometimes you just have to bear it.

I also can't fight all of Brit's battles for her. Although I wish I could, that wouldn't be right, because it's not going to help her to stand up for herself. It's a lot like when there's a bully beating up on your child at school. Well, you know you just want to go set that little brat straight yourself—but you can't. You have to talk it over with your child, and you may have to help him or her confront it (or else talk to the teacher or that bully's mama).

It's fun to dress up, but I like to kick back and just relax, too. It can be exhausting dancing and singing all day.

I would always tell my kids that you should feel sorry for the people who pick on you—they're so jealous or insecure that they have to make you feel smaller so they can feel bigger. And that is sad.

Jealousy is a terrible emotion—it can only be destructive. No matter how little I had, no matter how bad times were for our family, I never once was jealous of other people who had more. I was always happy for them and always wished them well. My children have grown up supporting one another as well—neither Jamie Lynn nor Bryan is ever jealous of Britney's success. They love her and are thrilled for her and are so, so proud. The only time my kids get jealous is when they think I'm favoring one over the other: Bry always says, "You always pay attention to Britney," and Britney always says, "You dote on Bryan." And Jamie Lynn—well, she just wants attention twenty-four hours a day and whines when she doesn't get it! But you know I love them all the same, with all my heart.

"*I expected Britney would be famous one day—but not this young. I thought maybe by age twenty-five she'd have an album out there, but she's exceeded all of our wildest expectations. This has been life-changing for us.*" —Bryan Spears, big brother

# The Pressure Mounts

People ask me a lot if I'm worried that my career won't last. Not really. With the next album, of course, there's pressure to prove I can do it again. My first album sold more than 11 million copies in the United States alone. That's hard to top. But look at the Backstreet Boys. Critics said, "They'll be just a flash in the pan," but they came out with their second album and it was just as great. What it boils down to is the music: I have an amazing team of writers, musicians, and producers, and they are churning out great songs for me. I also look at it this way: if your fans like you, they want you to grow, and they'll grow with you. So what do I have to worry about? I know I have the best fans in the world! ✢

# Endless Interviews

Poor Brit. Talking about herself is probably her least favorite thing (that's her little-girl shyness again), but because she's now a public figure, she's expected to do the talk shows and chat with everyone from Diane Sawyer to Rosie O'Donnell. The hardest shows for her to do are the morning ones, *Good Morning America* and *The View*. Brit has such a hard time getting out of bed before noon. (If you were in the studio until 3 A.M., you would, too!) She has to really make an effort to get her voice opened up that early. She sits in the greenroom, making all these funny howling and screaming noises until she's warmed up. It's her own brand of vocal exercise. I can't even begin to describe it except to say it sounds awful! But folks have to do what works for them.

Brit has a hard time watching herself on TV, too. She'll always call me and say, "What did I say? I was so nervous, I can't remember what came out of my mouth when Joy Behar asked me that question about President Clinton!" Not to worry. She always does us proud. ✢

# The Price of Fame

Once, early on, Fe and I were at MTV in New York and the fans mobbed us so that we couldn't move in any direction. We were shoved up against a brick wall. That was very scary. Although no one meant to harm us, we could have been crushed in the crowd. Ever since that day, we've had Big Rob with us for security. He looks tough, but he's really a teddy bear around me. It was hard at first to get used to someone following us everywhere we went. I like to go where I want, when I want. But I realize that sometimes I need Rob's protection, and now I think of him as a buddy, not a bodyguard. When you become a star, you do lose a lot of your ability to just be a person. You can't go to the mall alone or take a stroll down the street. I could probably cause a little bit of a commotion now if I went to the Wal-Mart back home. You do have to sacrifice your freedom when you're in this business, but it's a small price to pay for all the good. ❁

# The Ups and Downs

Achieving your goal is a wonderful thing, and you should be very proud when you do. But it doesn't mean that everything is going to be perfect from that moment on. Most people expect paradise, and they set themselves up for a big disappointment. You have to be realistic and practical. No one's life, no matter how rich or famous they are, is without difficulties. We're all human! Of course you want to encourage your child to succeed, but you should also warn them gently that success isn't everything and it does come with its very own set of problems. I never have to remind Brit of this, because she's so well-grounded; she understands that in the end, it's people, not things, that matter most. Being in this business for a while, we've all seen what success can do to people. It can go to your head (Brit hates when people act stuck up); it can destroy you (especially when it suddenly disappears and you didn't anticipate it). I think it's important to prepare your child to cope with what her success will mean. Let's say she wants to win the school spelling bee; then the state one; then the national. Well, that's a great goal to set, but does she understand that winning will place her in the spotlight (all those newspapers and TV reporters), possibly cause other kids in school to resent her, and pile on more pressure than she's ever experienced? Just lay it all out for your child: "Baby, this could happen, and just be ready in case it does." Then assure your child that, come what may, you'll deal with it together. ❁

*I feel so much better knowing that Big Rob is on the road with Britney.*

I have had so much fun this year. I've gotten to hang out with Melissa Joan Hart, the star of *Sabrina, the Teenage Witch*. I appeared on her show once, and she was in my video for "Crazy."

This is Britney in the studio for her first album. She loves everything about making albums, and I know she has big plans for her future as a singer!

# She Did It Again

Like we said, Britney and I were never big on planning. But hopes and dreams are plans in their own way. They're your vision of what you'd like tomorrow to hold, and you work toward that vision. It's important to encourage your child to think about the future. You certainly don't have to make a checklist of what it will include, but isn't it fun to imagine it? Britney is always dreaming. You'd think that she'd stop now that she's gotten this far, but nuh-uh!

She has more and more opportunities opening up to her every day: movie scripts, duets, appearances, endorsements. It's so hard to choose, much less squeeze things into her schedule. She wants to act in movies—a teen one, maybe, that's fun and appropriate for her age. She was on *Sabrina, the Teenage Witch* with her friend Melissa Joan Hart, and there was talk of a guest spot on her favorite show, *Dawson's Creek*. They were all set to have her film a role, but Britney couldn't fit it in (she was making a video). The producers say she's still welcome, so maybe next time.

Her second album will be even better than the first—and that's not just a proud mama talking. Everyone who's heard it says so. I heard Brit's new single "Oops!…I Did It Again" for the first time while I was working on this book at our publisher's office in New York City. Brit's manager, Larry Rudolph, brought it over for me to hear on a boom box. I held my breath and watched the reaction of everyone else in the room. They were tapping their feet and really getting into it. I don't know why, but I always get so nervous the first time I hear one of her songs. I loved this one right away—I think it's got the most incredible beat, and Brit's voice sounds great. But my palms always get sweaty because I know how hard she's worked and I want it to be incredible.

I know Brit's very excited about "Oops!" Usually, you ask her how a song is and she says, "You know, it's good, it's good." This time, she said, "Mama, it is the *ultimate*!" Which I think is as good as it gets!

She's loving every minute of the creative process and hardly realizes how hard she's been working. I don't think it's work to her at all—it's pure joy. But even once the album is "put to bed" (as she'll call it), her job is far from over. Then comes shooting the videos and promoting and touring. Along with promoting the album, we'll be out there talking about our book. And I must admit, that was another one of my motivations in writing it—I just wanted to be with Brit! ✽

*I can't wait to make more videos for my new album, **Oops!... I Did It Again**. Here I am with Melissa Joan Hart in the "Crazy" video from ...**Baby One More Time**.*

Mama and I can be such girls together. We loved going through my gifts at the party for my eighteenth birthday.

# One More Time

I cannot believe this is my second CD already! It seems like only yesterday I was recording my very first album. The time has flown by so quickly, and I know the next year will be even busier than the last two. The second album's release date is May 16 and my concert tour kicks off in June, taking us to fifty-five cities around the country. What will make it even better is that my gang is all coming with me: Big Rob; Fe; my other manager, Johnny Wright, who handles my touring and shows while Larry handles the business side; eight dancers; five band members; and the crew. In total, we're about thirty-three people. That's a lot of bodies to pack into a few buses, which is how we travel. I know seeing the country by bus doesn't sound too comfy, but it's actually great. Like a great big slumber party! We have bunk beds and it's very luxurious, so sleeping (my number one priority) is easy.

This album is similar in style to my first—a lot of pop music that just makes you feel good and want to get on your feet and dance. But hold on to your seats for the third one. I think it will be a change—definitely more of a stretch for me creatively. Believe it or not, I kind of see myself one day going more into ballads and R&B (that's really my sound). I write songs, too (I had a whole book of lyrics, but Jamie Lynn has gone and hid it somewhere!), and I want to record them.

And yes, I want to make movies. I enjoyed acting in *Ruthless!* and in skits on the *Mickey Mouse Club*, so I'd like fans to see that side of me, too. I'm waiting for the perfect project to come along, something that just grabs me instantly. I'll know it when I see it. That's the way it's always been, and my instincts haven't failed me yet.

I've been asked by a lot of reporters what I'm going to do with all the money I make, and I always say the same thing: I guess I'll save it for when I need it. You never know when a rainy day might come along out of nowhere. My family's had its share of rainy days, maybe even a few major thunderstorms, so I'm real cautious.

When I became a success, it wasn't like it was just given to me overnight, so I appreciated it that much more. I don't understand stars who spend a fortune on fancy cars and clothes and jewelry for themselves. If I were a trillionaire, I would still not go out and buy myself a yacht. What I would buy is nice things for my family and friends. Mama is at the top of that list, because she's the best and she always put us kids before her needs. She still does that. She'll call me up feeling totally guilty that she went out and bought one pair of pants at The Limited because they were cute. She'll say, "Oh, Britney, I really didn't need them, I shouldn't have!" That's the way we are, because all our lives we never knew what it was like to have money, or an abundance of anything. I remember how hard that was, and how bad it made us feel sometimes when there was so little in the refrigerator or our car kept breaking down. So with everything I earn now, I am ten times more grateful for it and for the security I know it gives us. Hopefully, there'll never be another time when we have bills we can't pay.

This year, we started building a new house for my mama on seven acres of beautiful land in Kentwood. I also bought her a new car. You should have seen her face when I handed her the keys to a shiny new Mercedes for Christmas. I take such great pride in being able to do that for her, although she has a hard time accepting it. She says, "Brit, you don't have to pay me back for anything. That's what mamas are for." I don't *have* to, I *want* to. And my other siblings feel the same way: Bryan will go out of his way to bring Mama piping-hot biscuits from the bakery on a Sunday morning, and Jamie Lynn always announces that she'll buy Mama the moon and the stars as soon as she gets to be rich and famous! ✿

# It's Better to Give Than to Receive

I raised my kids to understand the importance of generosity and charity, and now, I'm proud to say, they never need reminding. It's children that touch Britney's heart the most. This year, right before Christmas, she asked to visit Children's Hospital in Baton Rouge. (Her friend Cindy works there in the oncology unit.) She saw all these terminally ill kids and she brought them bears and dolls and played with them. Then they asked her if she wanted to go into the critical care unit and, bless her heart, she said, "Sure, yeah," not knowing what she would see. Inside, she met a little boy who was no more than about three years old, and he was lying there with all of these machines and tubes, barely breathing. His parents were standing over him, holding his hand and praying for him to be at peace. Well, Britney just started to cry. She ran into the bathroom and I went into check on her. She said, "Mama, I am so sorry. I shouldn't have done that in front of that mom and dad." She came out and apologized, and this couple was so moved by her. Then she sat down and held that little boy's hand, too, and she smiled and put on a brave face for him.

There's another little boy, a six-year-old in New York, who says he's Brit's biggest fan. He has leukemia, and he was supposed to have died the week of Christmas. That's how bad off he was. Brit calls him and writes to him all the time, and she came to see him around the holidays. Well, do you know that his blood count went up right after she visited? The doctors could not believe it. He's still hanging in there, and it's absolutely a miracle. Britney carries his picture with her everywhere she goes. She says it reminds her of how precious life is and why she was given the gifts she has—so she could use them to help others.

She's starting an arts camp this summer for inner-city kids, and she's getting involved in St. Jude's Children's Hospital. I know Britney, and it's just the beginning. She has big plans.

The Giving Back Fun

*I have always taught my kids that you have to give back to others less fortunate than you are, and Britney has taken this to heart. Here she is with her managers Johnny Wright (left) and Larry Rudolph (right) at a press conference they did for her charity.*

I'm proud of everything my daughter does, but I'm most proud of what a good and kind person she is. I think the only way to teach a child charity is to set a good example yourself. I always pitched in around our community and at the church, and always took my kids along to help. I believe that everyone is God's child and deserves the same love and understanding. Some people have less, some have more; some are healthy, some are sick. But we all are the same in God's eyes. My sister, Sandra, has an autistic son, and God bless him, I think he showed us all how to open our hearts and be compassionate. I know Britney loved him and always reached out to him. She didn't see anything wrong with him at all. To her he was just special.

When I see Brit today, hugging a little one who's lost her hair from chemotherapy or telling a child who's virtually at death's door to hang in there and be strong, I know I have done my job as a mama. ❇

I love thinking about the future. How could I not? I have so many wonderful people in my life—family and friends and my dancers and my managers. And most important, I have Mama, who will always be there for me.

# Healing Hearts

It's an amazing feeling—maybe even more amazing than the feeling I get when I perform—to be able to make a difference in someone's life. I think it has to be one of the best parts of being a star, and it is also the biggest responsibility. If you can change things for the better, if you can brighten someone's world a little bit, you just want to spend every moment doing it. But I can't. There's only so much time in a day. I feel bad sometimes when someone asks me to visit him in the hospital and it's so far away that I can't. We get so many letters, so many requests, it breaks my heart. So I try to do as much as I can. And I want to do even more in the future. There are lots of events and projects I want to be involved with personally. I could give money to a cause, but that doesn't seem like enough. I want to give more of myself, and I've told everyone I work with that we have to make the time because it's so important to me. I think maybe this is part of what God meant for me to do when I became successful. ❈

# Prize Winner

Britney's been recognized with a lot of awards and nominations lately (Billboard, MTV Europe, the People's Choice, American Music, the Grammys). I'm thinking I'll need a whole room to showcase them in the new house (and Jamie Lynn is quickly catching up with her own). Winning isn't everything, but it sure feels good, especially when your peers and your public recognize how hard you've worked. I watched the American Music Awards on TV when they announced her nomination for Best New Pop Recording Artist, and I kept saying over and over again in my mind, "Let it be, let it be, let it be." Well, I guess God heard me, because she won. I was so happy, I wanted to do backflips myself! I have no doubt in my mind that there will be much more acclaim down the road for her, but what matters most is the fact that she is loving every moment of her life. And to think she's so young and she has a whole lifetime in front of her. The sky's the limit. Brit asked me to be her date for the Grammy Awards ceremony, and I was so thrilled. I tried to be really calm and cool for her. I didn't want her to see how nervous I was about the awards, because then she'd be nervous, too. "Baby," I told her, "if it's meant to be, then it's meant to be. There's always next time."

I wouldn't begin to guess what Britney's future will hold. (I never underestimate my little girl!) It's always been up to her. But what I pray is that, whatever she does, it brings her happiness. I always tell her, "Brit, I'm proud of you no matter what." If she gave it all up tomorrow and decided she wanted to raise ten kids on a farm in Louisiana, I'd be proud of her. In fact, if she moved back home, I'd be thrilled!

I expect our relationship will change. Britney is growing up so fast, and I know one day she won't need her mama like she used to. I guess she already doesn't! That's okay, because it's how it should be. We'll have new things to talk about, new things to share. Does it make me a little sad that my baby is not a baby anymore? Well, sure it does, because I remember changing her diapers and cradling her in my arms. But I cannot wait for her to experience those powerful feelings of love herself (and that means she has to grow up). Every mama has mixed emotions when her little girl becomes a woman. It's natural. The trick is to find new ways to relate to each other—maybe not as child and parent anymore, but as friends. Time, distance, and change don't have to drive you apart. They can bring you closer together. ❁

# Settling Down

There might come a day (although it's a long way off!) when performing won't be my top priority and raising a family will. I know I'll always have music in my life, whether it's singing or writing or even producing, but I think it's really important when you have a family that you're there with your kids. Those are the little moments that make life so special. I know a lot of people in the entertainment industry who have their kids on tour with them—and if they can work it out, that's cool, that's fine. But I just know the way I was brought up, and I would prefer them to be in more of a home environment—something more stable than being on a bus! I want to be the kind of mom my mama was for me. (And I bet she'll make an amazing grandma.)

Every lesson she taught me—about what it is to be a good and kind person, about never losing hope even when there doesn't seem to be any hope left—those are the things I want to hand down to my children one day.

I'd like my kids to one day read this book and realize how many people—my mama, especially—helped me to get to where I am. And if I'm real lucky, there are a lot more chapters in my story still to come. You know I can't wait to fill them.

And Mama—she'll be encouraging me to turn those pages, one by one. ❁

"Britney hasn't even begun to show the world what she can do yet." —Larry Rudolph, manager

## Arnold Turner photos

Text: 57, 58, 70, 81, 84, 90, 94, 100, 110, 112, 114, 115, 119, 123, 126, 127, 128, 131, 132, 135
Insert: 1; 4, 5, 11, 12, 14, 16

## Felicia Culotta photos

Text: 85, 87, 89, 94, 96, 99, 104, 106, 124
Insert: 6–7, 9, 13

## Photos courtesy of the authors

Text: 6, 7, 9, 16, 18, 24, 28, 30, 31, 34, 38, 40, 41, 42, 47, 49, 50, 51, 52, 61, 62, 64, 69, 72, 76, 77, 82, 92
Insert: 2, 3, 6, 8, 9, 10, 11